DEPARTMENT OF THE ENVIRONMENT

The Potential for Woodland Establishment on Landfill Sites

M C Dobson and A J Moffat

The Forestry Authority
Research Division

LONDON: HMSO

ISBN 0 11 752678 9

KEYWORDS: Forestry, Landfill, Reclamation, Tree establishment, Tree roots

This report is one of a series within the Controlled Waste Management Research and Development Programme (Ref: CWM 054/92)

Enquiries relating to this publication should be addressed to:

Minerals and Land Reclamation Division or
Wastes Technical Division,
Department of the Environment
2 Marsham Street, London, SW1P 3EB

or

Technical Publications Officer,
The Forestry Authority,
Forest Research Station,
Alice Holt Lodge, Wrecclesham,
Farnham, Surrey, GU10 4LH

Front cover: Alder, ash, cherry mixed woodland over landfill, six years after planting into soil placed by loose-tipping. *Inset*: Unloading of waste, and spreading with steel-wheeled compactor.

Acknowledgements

This study was jointly commissioned by the Minerals and Land Reclamation Division and Wastes Technical Division of the Department of the Environment. We are particularly grateful to Dr T. Simpson (DoE Minerals and Land Reclamation Division), the Department's Nominated Officer, and to the Steering Committee for their helpful guidance: Miss A. Ward (Chair, DoE Minerals and Land Reclamation Division); Mr A. Bawa (Secretary, DoE Minerals and Land Reclamation Division); Mr P. Tempany (DoE Wastes Technical Division); Mrs C. Davis (DoE Directorate of Rural Affairs); Mr P.E. Gawn (British Aggregate Construction Materials Industries); Mr J. Pentlow (Association of County Councils); Mrs E. Simmons (Standing Local Authority Officers Panel on Land Reclamation); Mr R. Mould (Sand and Gravel Association); Mr I. Lanyon (British Aggregate Construction Materials Industries) and Mr J. Warren (National Association of Waste Disposal Contractors).

We would also like to thank colleagues in the Forestry Authority Research Division; Dr M.P. Coutts for reviewing Chapter 3, Mr C.P. Quine for reviewing Chapter 4, and Dr T.R. Nisbet for reviewing Chapter 5. We are very grateful to the phototypesetting staff of the Forestry Commission for preparation of the text, and to George Gate and John Williams for production of the illustrations.

Bibliographic Database:

Over 500 references were consulted during the compilation of this review. These have been incorporated into a stand-alone package based on Fox Pro 2.0, which allows searching of the data by author(s), Keyword(s) and reference number. Each entry has full bibliographic details, and over 350 are accompanied by a substantial summary. Further details and costs can be obtained from:

Environmental Consultancy
University of Sheffield
PO Box 595
Sheffield
S10 2UJ   Tel: 0742 768555

Contents

The Potential for Woodland Establishment on Landfill Sites

Executive Summary

There are approximately 136 million tonnes of controlled waste generated annually in the UK, and over 90% of this is landfilled in the 4000 or so sites currently licenced to accept waste. Most sites were previously used for mineral extraction, though some non-mineral sites are also landfilled. As well as being a valuable source of income, landfilling can serve as part of the strategy for restoring sites to a beneficial land use. For many sites, especially those used for mineral extraction, infilling with waste is the only way to enable restoration to appropriate levels, and with a landform which fits into the surrounding landscape.

The continued acceptance of landfill as a waste disposal option depends primarily on the ability to prevent pollution of the environment, and to achieve a restored landscape that is aesthetically acceptable. The former objective is usually achieved by containment of the waste, i.e. sealing the base and sides, and capping the top of the site with impermeable materials, combined with leachate and gas management systems. The latter objective is achieved by planting appropriate vegetation in the soil overlying the cap. However, since 1986 flexibility in landscaping restored sites has been considerably reduced as a result of guidance contained in the Department of the Environment's Waste Management Paper No. 26, *Landfilling Wastes*. This recommends that trees should not be planted on containment landfill sites.

The recommendation against tree planting centred principally on the perception that tree roots could penetrate into and through the landfill cap. They might thus compromise control of water ingress into waste and increase leachate generation. On clay capped sites, it was thought that tree roots could extract moisture from the clay and cause shrinkage and desiccation cracking. Concern was also expressed that if tree roots were to penetrate through the cap they would suffer owing to the high concentrations of landfill gas and elevated temperatures within the waste. In addition, trees on landfill sites were considered to be particularly susceptible to windthrow because a wind-firm root system was not expected to develop on the relatively shallow depth of soil above the cap. This would be a problem if upheaval of soil cover in the root plate of windblown trees resulted in exposure of the cap.

As a result of this guidance, and the earlier perceptions about trees which prompted it, virtually no modern capped landfill sites have been planted with trees. However, there is now an increasing awareness of the value of woodland both for landscape and conservation reasons. A study was therefore commissioned by the Department of the Environment in June 1991 to examine whether, and under what circumstances, woodland could be established on containment landfill sites.

Information was gathered through an extensive literature review complemented by consultations with the waste disposal industry, waste regulation authorities, mineral planning authorities, foresters, and specialist scientists involved in landfill and forestry research. A number of landfill sites restored to a woodland afteruse were visited and the relative success or failure of establishment was assessed. On some sites, representative trees were excavated to enable investigations of tree root distribution in landfill cover soils. The project was guided by a steering group made up of representatives from the DoE, mineral planning authorities, and the minerals and waste disposal industries.

The information presented in this report focuses primarily on the effects of the landfill environment on tree growth, the typical rooting pattern of trees, the likelihood of windthrow, and the possible effects of trees on landfill hydrology, as these are the main areas of concern highlighted in Waste Management Paper No. 26.

Landfill gas, leachate and high temperatures can all affect tree performance and survival. However, these factors are not considered to be particularly important in determining tree growth on well-engineered containment sites. On such sites, contamination of the root zone by landfill gas and leachate is prevented by the cap, which also serves to attenuate the elevated temperatures found within the waste. Factors such as soil compaction, water-logging, drought, shallow soil and poor soil quality are more likely to be of greater importance in determining the success of woodland establishment on capped sites.

A review of the rooting patterns of woodland trees revealed, contrary to popular belief, that trees are typically relatively shallow-rooted rather than deep-rooted. Maximum depths achieved by tree roots are most often between 1 and 2 m. Somewhere in the region of 90% of tree roots, and virtually all the larger roots, are to be found in the upper 1 m of soil.

The depth of soil explored by tree roots is limited principally by unfavourable soil conditions. Thus, tree roots do not grow into soils which are excessively compact, anaerobic (waterlogged), dry, or infertile. A clay cap, which combines a high degree of compaction, anaerobic conditions and infertility, will therefore present an effective barrier to vertical root growth. Roots will not grow through synthetic capping materials such as high density polyethylene (HDPE).

Trees growing on landfill sites with a depth of rootable soil of 1 m or more are unlikely to be at greater risk from windthrow than most forest trees on undisturbed sites. Nevertheless, techniques are available to quantify the potential windthrow hazard for particular sites, and these involve assessing the windiness of the local climate, elevation, topographical exposure and rooting depth. The risk of windthrow can be reduced by encouraging deeper rooting, which enhances stability, by planting trees which are relatively small at maturity, or by managing woodland under the coppice system.

Tree roots are not considered to be a primary cause of desiccation cracking in a clay cap. This is because at the bulk densities usually found in a compacted clay cap (>1.8 g cm^{-3}), maximum potential shrinkage is restricted to about 1.5–6.5%, and this is achieved only if all the moisture has been removed. Tree roots are only able to extract approximately 25% of total moisture, and this is insufficient to cause the level of shrinkage normally associated with cracking. Nevertheless, further field data on the shrinkage behaviour of clay caps is desirable.

Closed canopy woodland, by intercepting rainfall on leaves and branches, is often capable of significantly reducing net rainfall compared to grassland or arable crops. In some situations, therefore, woodland may reduce percolation into a landfill site by reducing the amount of water entering cover soils.

The available evidence suggests that woodland can be successfully established on containment landfill sites without compromising pollution control measures. Nevertheless, in order to maintain the integrity of the cap, and to ensure good tree growth,

the highest standards of restoration practice should be observed. It is therefore recommended that landfill sites are sealed with a low permeability cap to prevent migration of landfill gas into the rooting zone of trees. A synthetic cap should be covered with at least 1 m of rootable soil or soil-forming materials. A mineral cap should be covered by 1.5 m or more of soil material. The soil cover should be placed by loose-tipping to minimise soil compaction. If loose-tipping is not possible, or if reconsolidation takes place after soil placement, the soil must be ripped to a depth of at least 0.6 m prior to tree planting.

Sufficient post-settlement gradients are necessary to encourage shedding of surface water and to minimise soil waterlogging. For a forestry afteruse gradients of 1 in 10 are preferred, especially if soils are heavy. A coarse drainage layer placed directly above the cap will allow more rapid shedding of water and will greatly reduce percolation. It will also help to prevent roots from coming into contact with the cap.

If large amounts of settlement are predicted, tree planting should be delayed for some years. This will enable remedial filling to be carried out and will allow unhindered access for pipework and headgear maintenance. Planning conditions should ensure that the formal 5 year aftercare period (Planning and Compensation Act 1991) does not begin until remedial works have been carried out and the site is in a suitable state for tree establishment.

Selection of trees for planting on landfill sites must ensure that tree species are matched to particular site conditions. Nursery transplants or containerised stock should be used for woodland establishment as larger plants are generally unsuitable. Correct planting procedure, efficient weed control, and protection from browsing animals are also essential components of successful woodland establishment.

Woodland, once established, should be managed to enhance its economic, social, or wildlife benefits, depending on the planned objectives. Neglected woodland will tarnish the reputation of landfill as a disposal option, while well-managed and attractive woodland can help to win the goodwill of the waste regulation authorities and the general public alike.

Das Potential zur Afforstung auf Mülldeponien

Exekutivzusammenfassung

Jährlich fallen in dem UK etwa 136 Mio Tonnen kontrollierter Müll an und über 90% davon wird in ca.4000 zugelassenen Mullgruben deponiert. Die meisten Deponien wurden vorher zur Mineralgewinnung benutzt, obwohl auch andere Gelände gefüllt werden Mülldeponien können sowohl eine wertvolle Einkommensquelle sein, als auch Teil einer Strategie, den positiven Nutzen eines Geländes wiederherzustellen. Für viele Plätze, besonders solche die zum Mineralabbau benutzt wurden, ist Auffüllung mit Müll die einzige Möglichkeit, angemessene Niveaus und eine in die Landschaft passende Landform wiederherzustellen.

Um Deponien als Müllbeseitigungsmethode weiterhin akzeptabel zu machen, ist es wichtig, Umweltverschmutzung zu verhindern und eine aesthetisch akzeptable Landschaft wiederherzustellen. Das erstere wird durch Einschluß des Mülls erreicht, d.h.Versiegelung des Bodens und der Seiten und die Abdeckung mit wasserundurchlässigen Materialien, verbunden mit Sickerungs- und Gashandhabungssystemen. Die zweite Objekive wird durch Bepflanzung mit geeigneter Vegetation über der Abdeckungskappe erreicht. Seit 1986 ist die Flexibilität der Landschaftsarchitektur für Deponien erheblich reduziert worden, infolge von Richtlinien im Müllmanagment Papier No. 26 des Umweltministeriums- *Landfilling Wastes*. Dies rät daß Bäume nicht auf eingeschloßenen Deponien gepflanzt werden sollten.

Die Richtlinien gegen Baumpflanzung konzentrierten sich vor allem auf die Annahme, daß Baumwurzeln in und durch die Abdeckungsschicht dringen könnten. Sie könnten somit die Kontrolle von Wassereintritt in den Müll behindern und Sickerung erhöhen. Auf lehmbedeckten Geländen befürchtete man, daß Wurzeln dem Lehm Feuchtigkeit entziehen und dadurch Schrumpfung und Trockenrisse verursachen könnten. Es wurden auch Bedenken geäußert, daß Wurzeln, die durch die Kappe dringen, unter hohen Müllgaskonzentrationen und erhöhten Temperaturen leiden könnten. Es wurde zusätzlich angenommen, daß Bäume auf Deponien besonders windwurfanfällig sind, da es nicht zu erwarten war, daß sich in dem relativ seichtem Boden über der Kappe ein windfestes Wurzelsystem entwickeln kann. Dies würde zu einem Problem, falls durch den Erdumsturz im Wurzelteller gefallener Bäume die Kappe freigelegt würde.

Aufgrund dieser Richtlinien und der Beobachtungen von Bäumen, die sie veranlassten, sind so gut wie keine modernen Deponien mit Bäumen bepflanzt worden. Man ist sich jetzt jedoch erhöht des Wertes von Wäldern für Landschafts- und Umweltschutzzwecke bewußt. Daher wurde im Juni 1991 vom Umweltministerium eine Studie in Auftrag gegeben, um zu untersuchen, ob und unter welchen Umständen Wälder auf eingeschloßenen Deponien angelegt werden könnten.

Information wurde durch eine unfangreiche Literaturprüfung sowie durch Konsultationen mit der Müllbeseitigungsindustrie, Müllüberwachungsbehörden, Mineralienplanungsbehörden, Waldarbeitern und Experten in der Müll- und Forstwissenschaft gesammelt. Eine Anzahl von Mülldeponien die zur Waldnutzung rekultiviert wurden, sind besucht worden und der relative Erfolg oder Mißerfolg der Aufforstung wurde bewertet. Auf einigen Geländen wurden repräsentative Bäume ausgegraben, um die Baumwurzelverteilung im Abdeckboden zu untersuchen. Das Projekt wurde von einer Gruppe geleitet, die sich aus Repräsentanten des Umweltministeriums, der Planungsbehörden und der Mineralien- und Müllbeseitigungsindustrie zusammensetzte.

Die Information die in diesem Bericht präsentiert wird, konzentriert sich vor allem auf den Einfluß der Müllumgebung auf den Baumwuchs, die typische Wurzelbildung der Bäume, die Wahrscheinlichkeit von Windwurf und die möglichen Einflüße von Bäumen auf den Deponienwasserhaushalt, da dies die Hauptgründe für Beunruhigung im Müllmanagment Papier No. 26 waren.

Müllgas, Sickerung und hohe Temperaturen können alle Baumleistung und -überleben beeinflußen. Diese Faktoren werden jedoch auf gut geplanten, geschloßenen Deponien nicht als besonders wichtig für das Baumwachstum angesehen. Auf solchen Plätzen wird eine Verseuchung der Wurzelzone durch Müllgas und Sickerung durch die Kappe verhindert, welche auch die im Müll entstandenen, hohen Temperaturen verringert. Faktoren wie etwa Bodendichte, Wassersättigung, Dürre, seichter Boden und schlechte Bodenqualität sind wahrscheinlich viel entscheidender am Erfolg einer Waldetablierung auf bedeckten Plätzen.

Eine Überprüfung der Wurzelbilder von Waldbäumen ergab, daß sie, entgegen allgemeiner Meinung, eher flach als tief verwurzelt sind. Die Maximaltiefen, die von Wurzelsystemen erreicht werden, sind meist zwischen 1 und 2 Metern.

Ungefähr 90% der Wurzeln und fast alle größeren Wurzeln können im obersten Meter des Bodens gefunden werden. Die Tiefe des Bodens die von Baumwurzeln erforscht wird, wird vor allem durch ungünstige Bodenbedingungen begrenzt. Somit wachsen Wurzeln nicht durch Böden die ausgesprochen dicht, anaerob, trocken oder unfruchtbar sind. Eine Lehmkappe, welche Dichte, Luft- und Wasserundurchlässigkeit sowie Unfruchtbarkeit miteinander verbindet, stellt somit eine effektive Barriere gegen senkrechten Wurzelwuchs dar. Wurzeln wachsen nicht durch synthetische Deckmaterialien wie etwa schweres Polyethyl (HDPE).

Bäume, die auf Deponien mit einer zu bewurzelnden Rekultivierungsschict von einem Meter oder mehr wachsen, sind wahrscheinlich nicht einem größerem Windwurfrisiko ausgesetzt, als Bäume auf ungestörtem Gelände. Es gibt jedoch Prozeduren um das Windwurfpotential einzelner Gelände zu meßen, diese beinhalten Beurteilung des lokalen Windaufkommens, der Höhenlage, der topographischen Lage und der der Wurzeltiefe. Das Windwurfrisiko kann durch die Förderung tieferer Wurzelsysteme, welche Stabilität vergrößern, durch die Pflanzung von Baumarten die in der Reife relativ klein sind oder durch die Pflege als Niederwald verringert werden.

Baumwurzeln werden nicht als eine Hauptursache für Trockenrisse in Lehmkappen angesehen. Der Grund dafür ist, daß bei der Dichte die normalerweise in verdichteten Lehmkappen vorhanden ist (>1.8 g cm^{-3}) die maximal mögliche Schrumpfung auf etwa 1.5–6.5% begrenzt ist und dies nur wenn alle Feuchtigkeit entzogen worden ist. Baumwurzeln sind aber nur fähig etwa 25% der vorhandenen Feuchtigkeit abzuziehen und dies ist ungenügend um den Außmaß vonSchrumpfung zu bewirken der normalerweise mit Rissen verbunden ist. Jedoch ist es wünschenswert weitere Daten über das Schrumpfverhalten von Lehmkappen zu erhalten.

Im Vergleich zu Weideland oder Getreide ist ein Wald mit geschloßenem Laubdach oft fähig die Nettoregenmenge, durch Auffang in Laub und Ästen, beträchtlich zu verringern. In manchen Umständen könnte Wald somit Durchsickern verringern, indem er die Wassermenge, die den Erdboden erreicht, reduziert.

Die verfügbaren Tatsachen deuten darauf hin, daß Wald auf eingeschloßenem Deponien erfolgreich etabliert werden kann, ohne Umweltschutzmaßnahmen zu gefährden. Um jedoch die Integrität der Kappe zu erhalten und einen guten Baumwuchs

sicherzustellen, sollten die höchsten Anforderungen an die Wiederherstellungspraktiken gestellt werden. Es wird hiermit geraten, daß die Deponien mit einer Kappe von geringer Durchlässigkeit versiegelt werden, um einen Austritt von Müllgas in die Wurzelzone zu verhindern. Eine synthetische Kappe sollte mit mindestens einem Meter Erdreich oder bodenformendem Material bedeckt werden. Eine Mineralkappe sollte mit 1.5 oder mehr Meter Bodenmaterial bedeckt werden. Die Rekultivierungsschicht sollte durch Aufschütten aufgetragen werden, um eine Bodenverdichtung zu vermeiden. Wo Aufschütten nicht möglich ist oder wo weitere Festigung nach Bodenauftrag auftritt, muß der Boden vor der Pflanzung auf mindestens 0.6 Meter Tiefe aufgebrochen werden.

Nach Senkung ist ein ausreichendes Gefälle nötig, um die Verteilung des Oberflächenwassers zu fördern und dadurch das Durchnässen des Erdbodens zu vermeiden. Für den forstwirtschaftlichen Gebrauch ist ein Gefälle von 1:10 wünschenswert, besonders bei schweren Böden. Eine Entwässerungsschict direktüber der Kappe hilft mit der Wasserverteilung und verringert Infiltration. Sie verhindert auch den Kontakt der Wurzeln mit der Kappe.

Falls viel Senkung erwartet wird, sollte Baumpflanzung um einige Jahre verzögert werden. Dies ermöglicht zusätzliche Auffüllungen und ungehinderten Zugang zur Rohr-und Leitungswartung. Planungsbedingungen sollten garantieren, daß die formelle 5 jährige Nachversorgungsperiode (Planning and Compensation Act 1991) erst nach Vollendung notwendiger Abhilfsmaßnahmen beginnt, wenn also das Gelände zur Aufforstung bereit ist.

Die Wahl der Baumarten zur Pflanzung auf Deponien hängt von der Brauchbarkeit unter den jeweiligen Geländebedingungen ab. Es sollten Baumschulsetzlinge oder kleine Containerpflanzen benutzt werden, da größere Pflanzen zur Aufforstung meist ungeeignet sind. Korrekte Pflanzprozeduren, effektive Unkrautbekämpfung und der Schutz vor äsenden Tieren sind unerläßliche Bestandteile einer erfolgreichen Aufforstung.

Das etablierte Waldgebiet sollte entsprechend seiner geplanten Objektiven gepflegt werden, um seinen wirtschaftlichen, sozialen oder natürlichen Nutzwert zu erhöhen. Vernachlässigte Wälder geben Deponien einen schlechten Ruf als Müllbeseitigungsmöglichkeit, während gut gepflegte und attraktive Waldgebiete sowohl die Müllplanungsbehörden als auch die Öffentlichkeit positiv beeinflußen können.

Les Possibilités Offertes par l'Implantation de Bois sur les Sites de Remblaie.

Resumé d'Exécution

Le Royaume-Uni produit chaque année près de 136 millions de tonnes de déchets sous contrôle, dont plus de 90% sont mises en remblaie dans les quelque 4000 sites actuellement autorisés à accepter les déchets. La majorité sont d'anciens sites d'extraction minière, bien qu'on remblaie aussi des sites à caractère non minier. Tout en étant une précieuse source de revenus, le remblaie peut aussi être utilisé dans le cadre de la stratégie visant à restituer ces sites à une utilisation rentable des terres. Pour un grand nombre d'entre eux, particulièrement ceux qui ont été utilisés pour l'extraction minière, le remplissage avec des déchets paraît être la seule façon dont on puisse leur redonner un niveau qui convient et un relief dont les formes s'harmonisent avec le paysage enironnant.

La persistance avec laquelle le remblaie continuera d'être accepté comme option d'évacuation des déchets dépend surtout de l'aptitude dont on fera preuve pour éviter la pollution de l'environnement et pour recréer un paysage qui soit acceptable sur le plan esthétique. Le premier objectif est généralement réalisé par l'isolation des déchets – en assurant l'étanchéité de la base et des côtés du site, puis en couvrant sa partie supérieure d'une calotte de matériaux imperméables – en même temps que l'utilisation de systèmes de gestion des composés lessivés et gaz. Le deuxième objectif est réalisé par la plantation d'une végétation appropriée dans le sol recouvrant la calotte. Néanmoins, depuis 1986, la flexibilité d'aménagement des sites réhabilités se trouve considérablement réduite du fait des recommandations contenues dans le numéro 26 du Waste Management Paper publié par le ministère de l'Environnement, qui s'intitule *Landfilling Wastes*. Il y est en effet recommandé de ne pas planter d'arbres sur les sites renfermant du remblaie en isolation.

Ces recommandations hostiles à la plantation d'arbres s'appuyaient principalement sur l'idée que les racines d'arbres pouvaient pénétrer dans la calotte recouvrant le remblaie et même la traverser. Il devenait donc possible qu'elles compromettent le contrôle de la pénétration de l'eau dans les déchets et accroissent la génération de composés lessivés. On pensait que, sur les sites fermés par une calotte d'argile, les racines d'arbres pouvaient extraire l'humidité de l'argile causant un retrait et l'apparition de fentes dues au dessèchement. On exprima aussi de l'inquiétude à l'idée que, si les racines d'arbres pénétraient au travers de la calotte, elles souffriraient des hautes concentrations de gaz

formées à l'intérieur du remblaie et des températures élevées, régnant au milieu des déchets. De plus, les arbres plantés sur les sites de remblaie étaient considérés comme étant particulièrement susceptibles d'être arrachés par le vent, parce qu'on ne s'attendait pas à ce qu'un réseau de racines capable de résister au vent, puisse se développer dans la couche de sol relativement peu épaisse se trouvant au dessus de la calotte. Ceci pouvait être source de problèmes, si, en s'abattant, les arbres soulevaient le sol de couverture avec le volume de leur racines pour révéler la calotte.

A la suite de ces recommandations et du fait des conceptions prévalant précédemment sur les arbres, conceptions qui sont à l'origine de ces recommandations, quasiment aucun site de remblaie moderne n'a été planté d'arbres. Néanmoins, on note maintenant une prise de conscience croissante de l'utilité des bois, à la fois au niveau du paysage et pour des raisons de conservation. Le Ministère de l'Environnement britannique a donc demandé, en juin 1991, qu'une étude soit effectuée pour examiner s'il était possible d'implanter des bois sur les sites renfermant des déchets en isolation et quelles devaient être les conditions respectées par cette implantation.

Des informations ont été réunies grâce à un examen approfondi des documents s'y rapportant, que viennent compléter des consultations effectuées auprès de l'industrie de l'évacuation des déchets, des autorités de contrôle des déchets, des autorités de planification minière, des forestiers et des chercheurs spécialisés dans la sylviculture ou le remblaie. Un certain nombre de sites de remblaie qui ont été réhabilités etplantés de bois ont été visités pour évaluer le succès ou l'échec relatifs de cette implantation.

Dans certains sites, on a procédé au creusement de fosses au pied de certains arbres représentatifs pour permettre d'examiner la distribution de leurs racines à l'intérieur des sols recouvrant le remblaie. Le projet avait à sa tête une équipe de direction formée par des représentants du Ministère de l'Environnement britannique, des autorités de l'aménagement, des industries minières et des industries spécialisées dans l'évacuation des déchets.

L'information contenue dans ce rapport se concentre surtout sur les effets qu'a le milieu du remblaie sur la croissance des arbres et leur enracinement type, les probabilités de déracinement par le vent, ainsi que les effets que pourraient avoir les arbres sur l'hydrologie du remblaie, du fait que ces facteurs forment les principales zones d'inquiétude mises en lumiére dans le Waste Management Paper N° 26.

Les gaz, composés lessivés et hautes températures issus du remblaie sont tous en mesure d'avoir des répercussions sur le développement et la survie des arbres. Néanmoins ces facteurs ne sont pas considérés comme étant particulièrement importants lorsqu'il s'agit de déterminer la croissance des arbres sur les sites de mise en isolation bien conçus. Dans de tels sites, la contamination de la zone des racines par les gaz et composés lessivés issus remblaie est empêchée par la présence de la calotte qui sert aussi à atténuer les hautes températures trouvées dans les déchets. Il semble plus probable que des factuers tels que le compactage du sol, sa teneur excessive en eau, sa sécheresse, sa faible épaisseur et sa pauvreté jouent un rôle plus important pour déterminer le succès avec lequel les bois sont implantés sur les sites coiffés d'une calotte.

Une étude effectuée sur les types d'enracinements suivis par les arbres forestiers a révélé, contrairement à ce qu'on croit généralement, que les racines de ces derniers se développaient généralement en faible profondeur plutôt qu'en grande profondeur. Les profondeurs maximales réalisés par les réseaux d'enracinement des arbres sont le plus souvent entre 1 et 2 m. Environ 90% des racines d'arbres et quasiment toutes les racines les plus importantes se trouvent dans le premier mètre de profondeur. L'épaisseur de sol explorée par les racines d'abres est principalement limitée par les conditions défavorables du sol. Ainsi, les racines d'arbres ne développent pas dans les sols présentant un haut degré de compactage, des conditions anaérobies (une teneur excessive en eau) ou de l'infertilité. Une calotte d'argile combinant un fort degré de compactage, des conditions anaérobies et l'absence de fertilité formera donc une barrière efficace à la croissance verticale des racines. Ces dernières ne se développeront pas dans les calottes de fermeture en matériaux synthétiques tels que le polyéthylène de haute densité (HDPE).

Il est probable que les arbres poussant sur des sites de remblaie recouverts d'une couche de terre arable d'1 m ou plus, ne soient pas plus en danger d'être arrachés par le vent que la plupart des arbres forestiers poussant sur des sites intacts. Néanmoins, il existe des techniques permettant de quantifier les risques d'arrachage par le vent sur des sites particuliers, ces dernières nécessitent que l'on détermine la force des vents dans le climat local, l'élévation, l'exposition topographique et la profondeur d'enracinement. Le risque d'abattage par le vent peut être réduit lorsqu'on favorise une plus grande profondeur d'enracinement, qui donne plus de stabilité, en plantant des arbres dont la hauteur à maturité est relativement peu importante, ou en gérant les bois suivant le système du taillis.

On ne considère pas que les racines d'arbres soient une cause primordiale d'apparition de fentes de dessèchement sur les calottes d'argile. C'est parce que dans les densités généralement trouvées dans une calotte d'argile compactée ($>1,8$ g cm^{-3}), le retrait maximal pouvant survenir est réduit à environ 1,5–6,5%, il faut ajouter que ceci ne se produit que lorsque l'humidité a entièrement disparu. Les racines d'arbres ne sont en mesure d'extraire qu'environ 25% de l'humidité totale, ce qui est insuffisant pour causer le niveau de retrait normalement associé à l'apparition de fentes. Il serait néanmoins désirable d'obtenir d'autres données relevées sur le terrain pour compléter notre information sur le retrait affectant les calottes d'argile.

Par comparaison avec les prairies et les cultures arables, les bois fermés, parce que leurs branches et feuilles interceptent la pluie, sont souvent capables de réduire de manière significative la pluie excédentaire. Dans certaines situations, les bois peuvent donc réduire la percolation dans le site de remblaie en réduisant la quantité d'eau s'infiltrant dans les sols de couverture.

Les évidences fournies suggèrent que les bois peuvent être implantés avec succès sur les sites de remblaie en isolation sans compromettre les mesures visant au contrôle de la pollution, mais que les plus hautes normes devraient être observées dans la mise en pratique de cette réhabilitation afin de maintenir l'intégrité de la calotte et d'assurer le bon développement des arbres. Il est donc recommandé que les sites de remblaie soient coiffés d'une calotte à faible perméabilité afin d'empêcher la migration des gaz du remblaie vers de la zone d'enracinement des arbres. Les calottes synthétiques devraient être recouvertes par au moins un mètre de terre arable ou de matériaux propres à la formation de sol. Les calottes minérales devraient être recouvertes par au moins 1,5 m de terre. Le sol de couverture devrait être déposé sans être tassé, afin de minimiser son compactage. Lorsque le dépôt de terre non tassée ne s'avère pas possible et que la reconsolidation a lieu après le placement du sol, celui-ci doit être tranché sur une profondeur d'au moins 0,6 m avant la plantation des arbres.

Il est nécessaire d'avoir, après tassement, des pentes suffisantes pour faciliter l'écoulement de l'eau de surface et pour minimiser une teneur en eau excessive du sol. Lorsque le site doit ensuite être boisé, une pente de 10 pour cent est préférée, surtout si le sol est lourd. Une couche de matériaux grossiers servant au drainage, qui sera placée directement sur la calotte, encouragera l'écoulement d'eau et réduira la percolation, tout en empêchant les racines d'entrer en contact avec la calotte.

Lorsqu'on prévoit un fort tassement, la plantation d'arbres devrait être retardée de plusieurs années. Ceci permettra de procéder à des bouchages de réparation et d'avoir l'accès libre pour l'entretien des conduites et des installations de surface. Le planning devrait aussi stipuler que la période officielle de surveillance après-travaux longue de cinq ans (Planning and Compensation Act 1991) ne commence pas avant que les ouvrages de protection n'aient été achevés et que le site ne convienne à l'établissement de bois.

Lors de la sélection des arbres devant être plantés sur les sites de remblaie, il faut s'assurer que les espèces choisies conviennent aux conditions particulières au site. Ce sont des plants repiqués et semis en conteneurs qui devront être utilisés pour l'implantation des bois, car les plantes plus développées ne conviennent généralement pas. Le respect des règles de plantation, le contrôle efficace des mauvaises herbes et la protection des arbres contre les dégâts occasionnés par les animaux sont aussi des composantes essentielles de la bonne implantation des bois.

Les bois, une fois implantés devraient être gérés dans le but d'améliorer les avantages qu'ils apportent sur le plan économique et social ou au niveau de la faune et de la flore, suivant les objectifs prévus. Des bois négligés terniront la réputation du remblaie en tant qu'option offerte pour l'évacuation des déchets, tandis que de beaux bois bien gérés aideront à gagner la bienveillance des autorités assurant le contrôle des déchets tout autant que celle du grand public.

List of Tables

List of Figures

List of Plates

Centre pages

Chapter 1

Introduction

Background

1.1 Landfill is the most common form of waste disposal in the UK. There are presently approximately 4200 sites licensed to accept waste, and these receive about 136 million tonnes each year (DoE, 1992). Most landfilling currently occurs on sites previously used for mineral extraction, though some non-mineral sites are also landfilled. As well as being a valuable source of income, landfilling can serve as part of the strategy for restoring sites to a beneficial land use. This is because for many mineral sites, infilling with waste is the only way to enable restoration to appropriate levels, and with a landform which fits into the surrounding landscape. Approximately 10 000 ha of land affected by mineral workings were recorded as being dependent upon imported fill to achieve reclamation in England in 1988 (DoE, 1991a).

1.2 The establishment of some form of vegetation is a vital part of the restoration strategy for landfill sites (DoE, 1989). The choice of vegetation is especially important as it ultimately determines the appearance of a restored site and the way in which it fits into the wider landscape. However, the ability to produce a landscape which is aesthetically pleasing has often proved difficult because the use of woody vegetation, including trees, is currently discouraged on capped landfill sites. This is because the Department of the Environment's Waste Management Paper No. 26 *Landfilling Wastes* (DoE, 1986) has recommended that 'trees should not be allowed to grow on lined landfill sites or where water input is regulated by an impervious cap or membrane'. The reasons given for such guidance were:

- the perception that tree roots could penetrate through an engineered cap and would thus compromise control of water ingress into waste and allow escape of landfill gas,

- the possibility that shallow rooting in trees on landfill sites could increase the risk of

trees blowing over, thus disrupting pollution control measures, and

- the observation that conditions on landfill sites could adversely affect tree survival.

1.3 The outcome of guidance contained in Waste Management Paper No. 26 is that since 1986, very few containment landfill sites have been restored to woodland, despite increasing interest in permitting some forms of tree cover, especially for landscape reasons. More recently, however, the Department of the Environment has acknowledged that the recommendation for restricting tree planting on landfill sites was based on little field experience or scientific evidence. Guidance contained in the Department's Mineral Planning Guidance Note 7 (DoE, 1989) is more flexible. It suggests that tree planting would be acceptable provided the engineered cap covering the waste was adequately protected. However, little detail was given on what these protective measures might entail.

1.4 A comprehensive review of relevant information was seen as a first step to enable well-founded guidance to be issued on all aspects of woodland establishment on landfill sites: its appropriateness, and the nature of precautionary measures, should they be found necessary. Thus, in June 1991 the Department of the Environment's Minerals and Land Reclamation Division, in conjunction with the Wastes Technical Division, engaged the Forestry Commission Research Division as contractors to evaluate the potential for woodland establishment on landfill sites. The purpose of this review was to provide information to update guidance contained in Waste Management Paper No. 26 (DoE, 1986).

1.5 The aim of this research was to establish whether the reasons given for restricting tree planting on landfill sites were justified or not. It was therefore important to evaluate:

- the likely patterns of tree root growth on landfill sites,

1

- the ability of tree roots to penetrate a landfill cap,

- whether trees on landfill sites would be at risk from windthrow, and how great this risk would be, and

- whether trees can actually grow on the comparatively harsh environment of a landfill site.

1.6 These subject areas have been examined by a thorough review of relevant literature, complemented by consultations with the waste disposal industry, waste regulation authorities, mineral planning authorities and statutory consultees (e.g. NRA), foresters, and specialist scientists involved in landfill and forestry research. A number of landfill sites restored to a woodland afteruse were also visited and representative trees were excavated to assess rooting patterns. The review has been guided by a Steering Group representing the Department of the Environment, mineral planning and waste regulation authorities, and the waste disposal and minerals industries. The information resulting from this review and consultation exercise should enable those involved in landfill planning and operation to make more informed choices about the place of trees on capped landfill sites.

Overview of landfilling

Legal framework

1.7 At present, the main legislation which covers landfill planning, licensing, operation, restoration and aftercare is contained in the Town and Country Planning Act 1990 (as amended by the Planning and Compensation Act 1991) and the Control of Pollution Act 1974. The Control of Pollution Act 1974 will be largely superseded by the Environmental Protection Act 1990 from April 1993. The disposal of special waste (any controlled waste which consists of or contains substances which are 'dangerous to life') is also regulated under the Control of Pollution (Special Waste) Regulations 1980 (revision expected in 1993).

1.8 In the UK, new landfill projects require both planning permission and a waste management licence, obtained from the appropriate planning authority and waste regulation authority respectively. Planning permission is subject to conditions covering such matters as operating hours, general limits on waste types, total inputs, operating life-span, final restored contours, restoration, aftercare and afteruse. Modern permissions will include aftercare conditions which specify the steps to be taken to bring the land to the required standard for the specified afteruse, whether it be agriculture, amenity or forestry. Since the implementation of the Town and Country Planning (Minerals) Act 1981, mineral planning authorities have been able to stipulate a post-restoration aftercare period of five years for reclaimed mineral extraction sites. This provision was extended to cover sites used for waste disposal under the provisions of the Planning and Compensation Act 1991.

1.9 Waste management licences can only be issued where there is a valid planning permission. Conditions will also be attached to the licence and these are designed to avoid pollution of the environment or harm to human health, and to ensure that disposal takes place to the appropriate standards. Such conditions normally follow consultation with statutory consultees i.e. the National Rivers Authority and the Health and Safety Executive, but may also include other organisations such as the Countryside Commission, Ministry of Agriculture, Fisheries and Food, and the Forestry Authority.

1.10 Under the Environmental Protection Act 1990 (when implemented) licence holders will be required to manage the landfill after it is completed and restored until such a time as a certificate of completion is issued, i.e. when the regulation authority is satisfied that the landfill no longer has any potential to cause environmental pollution or harm to human health. It is thought likely that the period of management prior to a certificate of completion being issued may be upwards of 30 years (Keeble, 1991).

1.11 The European Community (EC) also plays a role in setting standards for waste management, and an EC directive (currently in its 6th draft), if ratified, is likely to require an aftercare period of 10 years, and monitoring of leachate and groundwater quality for at least 30 years. Financial and planning provision for a long period of management are therefore likely to be necessary. Indeed, Keeble (1991) expresses the view that responsible licence holders should assume that their liabilities will be for several decades. All afteruses with the potential to generate income could offset some of the costs of ongoing monitoring and management, and in this timescale a woodland or forestry afteruse may be an economically attractive proposition (see Chapter 7).

2

Waste composition

1.12 Most landfill sites receiving inert wastes (i.e. wastes that do not undergo any significant physical, chemical or biological transformations when deposited in a landfill; DoE, 1986) do not need to be capped and therefore the recommendation against tree planting does not apply to such sites. Current recommendations are targeted at landfill sites licensed to receive biodegradable controlled wastes. Controlled wastes are defined in the Environmental Protection Act 1990 as *domestic*, *commercial* and *industrial* waste. Domestic waste comes mostly from private homes and tends to consist of a large proportion of paper, packaging and kitchen waste. Commercial waste is from business premises and is mainly composed of paper and packaging. Industrial waste derives from factories and industry, particularly the construction industry, and can consist of a variety of waste from scrap metal and plastics to concrete, wood and earth. Approximately 136 million tonnes of controlled wastes were produced in the UK in 1991 (DoE, 1992), with about 90% of this going directly to landfill (DoE, 1990). The remainder may be treated in some way, e.g. incineration, though the residues of treatment also usually end up being landfilled.

1.13 The introduction of the Clean Air Act in 1956, combined with a widespread change from coal fires to gas and oil-fired central heating systems, has brought about a profound change in the composition of household waste. In 1936 dust and cinders accounted for about 60% of all household waste, whereas the corresponding figure in the 1980's was only about 10–15% (Finch and Bradshaw, 1990). During the same period the amount of putrescible material (vegetable matter, paper, cardboard etc.) increased from about 25% to 55%, and plastics from zero to about 10%. The increasing proportion of putrescible, organic material in waste has led to three main problems in restored landfills: leachate production, landfill gas generation and settlement. However, most of these problems can be minimised by good landfill design and engineering practice.

Landfill design and operation

1.14 Modern landfill sites receiving controlled wastes are designed in such a way as to minimise environmental pollution resulting from biodegradation of the deposited material. This often entails isolating the waste from its surroundings by means of impermeable or low permeability barriers (Figure 1.1). Such 'containment' involves sealing the base, sides and top of a landfill site, usually through the use of compacted clays, though other synthetic materials such as HDPE are sometimes used (DoE, 1986). The sequence of operations usually begins with sealing the base and sides of the site and possibly the installation of a leachate collection system. Waste is then brought onto the site and is commonly deposited in a series of prepared cells delimited by bunds. Cells are filled sequentially and this enables progressive filling and restoration of the site (Figure 1.1).

1.15 The deposited waste is usually spread and compacted using purpose-built steel-wheeled compactors (Plate 1). These machines, by virtue of the cleats in their wheels, can exert ground pressures of over 15 MPa (150 kg cm^{-2}). Correctly used compactors can achieve densities of waste in the region of 0.5–1.0 tonnes m^{-3} depending on the type of waste and depth of the site (the weight of the waste itself can cause compaction). By contrast, tracked dozers exert static ground pressures of only about 0.1 MPa (1 kg cm^{-2}) and thus do not compact waste very efficiently (RMC, 1987). The highest degree of compaction is achieved when refuse is spread and compacted in thin layers of not more than 30 cm thick – the so-called 'onion-skin' technique. The purpose of waste compaction is to minimise the occurrence of excessive settlement which can disrupt surface drainage and pollution control measures, and can hamper effective restoration of the site. Overall settlement of well compacted waste may be of the order of 10% whereas poorly compacted waste may have rates of settlement nearer to 20–30% (RMC, 1987).

1.16 Once all, or part, of a containment site has been filled to the required depth, the final cap is installed (Plate 2). This is an engineered layer designed to prevent infiltration of water into the site and uncontrolled escape of landfill gas. The cap is covered by a layer of soil or soil-forming materials provided for the establishment of vegetation. Where the engineered cap consists of compacted clay, the soil cover has the additional role of preventing drying or cracking of the clay. Waste Management Paper No. 26 (DoE, 1986) recommends that the engineered cap should be constructed of material having a permeability to water of 1 x 10^{-7} cm s^{-1} or less. Waste Management Paper No. 26 also recommends that, for natural materials, the thickness of the

3

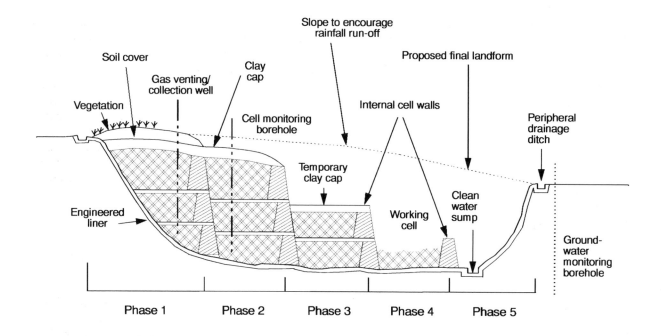

Figure 1.1 Schematic diagram (not to scale) to illustrate modern landfill site design (from DoE, 1986).

engineered cap should be about 1 m, and that the soil cover placed over the cap should be at least 1 m thick.

Pollution control

1.17 Unless a site is filled totally with inert waste containing no biodegradable material, the production of leachate and landfill gas, and to a greater or lesser degree, settlement, are inevitable. Leachate is the diverse mixture of dissolved and suspended organic and inorganic materials formed when the results of biodegradation mix with the downward migration of water through a landfill. Where it is permitted to escape into surface or groundwater it could seriously damage aquatic life, and could pollute water resources. It is principally because of the highly polluting nature of leachates that modern landfill sites are operated on containment principles. Indeed, in its consultation document *Policy and practice for the protection of groundwater* (NRA, 1991), the National Rivers Authority states that it will object to landfill sites which can be shown to present a risk of contamination to the water environment (within specified source protection zones) unless they are operated on containment principles and with an approved leachate management scheme.

Leachate treatment may consist simply of collection and disposal to foul sewer, or tankering away for sewage treatment. Alternatively it may involve on-site treatment by spray irrigation, re-circulation through the waste, or biological or chemical treatment (RMC, 1987).

1.18 Without proper management, the migration of landfill gas can give rise to risk of fire and explosion in nearby buildings, underground services or voids, and presents a risk of asphyxiation to animals, and death of plants. Containment therefore helps to prevent the uncontrolled migration of landfill gas away from the site or into cover soils. However, because the gas is contained it requires a system whereby it can be released into the atmosphere. This is commonly achieved by the installation of permeable trenches, gas drains installed within the landfill, or gas wells, similar in design to boreholes. The gas is then allowed to passively vent to atmosphere, or it is actively pumped. Pumped gas may be flared from a flarestack, or alternatively may be used as a source of fuel for heating or electricity generation (DoE, 1991b). Indeed, there is increasing interest in manipulating sites to enhance gas production where it is used for energy generation (Leach and Moss, 1989).

4

1.19 Gas combustion rather than passive venting is more environmentally acceptable because during combustion, methane (CH_4) is converted to carbon dioxide and water. This is good for two reasons: methane contributes significantly to the formation of the toxic air pollutant ozone, and methane is a more efficient 'greenhouse gas' than carbon dioxide and thus makes a greater contribution to climate change (Houghton *et al.*, 1990).

Why restore to woodland?

1.20 Aside from considerations of economics and availability of suitable land, the continued acceptability of landfilling as a disposal route for waste depends on two factors; the ability to prevent pollution of the environment, and the ability to restore sites to a beneficial afteruse. Through careful restoration of landfill sites, previously quarried or derelict land can be returned to a productive use, and can sometimes result in an improvement of the landscape. Now that restoration of landfill sites to agriculture is no longer seen as the high priority it used to be, and farmers are being encouraged to take land out of agricultural production, afteruses which include trees and woodland are being given much more serious consideration. Woodland is today regarded as a land use which has many benefits other than wood production. Trees can significantly improve the visual quality of the landscape, especially in areas where the site is open to frequent public view (Plates 3 and 4). The harsh profile of the 'bald green dome' typical of some landfill sites restored to grassland can be softened by the sensitive planting of woodland and hedgerows, allowing it to blend in with the wider landscape. In large phased sites woodland can provide screening for ongoing landfill activities (Plate 5) and can also provide a degree of shelter, especially important on exposed sites where windblown rubbish can be a problem.

1.21 Woods and hedgerows are increasingly viewed as important features for conservation as they provide valuable wildlife habitats, and can help to increase flora and fauna diversity. The creation of country parks on restored landfill sites is becoming a popular means of combining both conservation and recreation. Areas of woodland are seen more and more as important places for leisure-time activities, for walking, picnics, or for relaxation in pleasant surroundings. The creation of golf courses is also gaining popularity, and areas of trees and woodland are often seen as essential in providing an aesthetically pleasing and varied course.

1.22 In many cases restoration to woodland or nature conservation involving woody vegetation is the only sensible option on landfill sites where available soil cover may be poor both nutritionally and physically. Pioneer broad-leaved tree species such as alders are well suited to these conditions, and many conifers used in conventional forestry are also eminently suitable for growing on soils of low fertility. The potential for an economic forestry crop from such sites should not be underrated.

Summary

1.23 In June 1991 the Forestry Commission was engaged by the Department of the Environment to evaluate the potential for woodland establishment on landfill sites. The purpose of the exercise was to determine whether the presence of trees on capped landfill sites was likely to be detrimental to the maintenance of pollution control measures, and to determine whether trees could be successfully grown on landfill sites. Specifically, it was considered that tree roots might be able to penetrate through low permeability capping materials, and that comparatively shallow rooting of trees on landfill sites could result in an increased risk of trees being blown over in high winds, and consequent exposure of the cap (DoE, 1986). The following chapters are the culmination of an extensive literature review and consultation exercise, and are written with the intention of enabling planners and landfill operators to make an informed choice about the suitability of woodland as a restoration option.

1.24 Chapter 2 deals with the difficulties presented by landfill sites for woodland establishment, and their relative importance. Chapter 3 covers in some detail the rooting habit of trees, with the aim of providing an understanding of where tree roots grow in the soil and why. Chapter 4 details the factors influencing the stability of trees in strong winds, and outlines a site-specific system for classifying the risk of trees being blown over (Windthrow Hazard Classification). Chapter 5 assesses the effects trees are likely to have on the hydrology of a landfill site, and explores whether or not tree roots are likely to cause desiccation cracking of a clay cap. Chapter 6 draws together the findings of the previous chapters and provides recommendations for the successful establishment of trees on landfill sites. The economics of woodland establishment, and the financial implications of recommendations contained in Chapter 6, are considered in Chapter 7. Overall conclusions about woodland establishment on landfills are presented in Chapter 8.

Chapter 2

Landfill environment and tree growth

Introduction

2.1 Landfill sites can often provide an extremely inhospitable environment for tree growth. This is especially true of older sites where the standards of restoration and pollution control were much lower than those expected of modern sites under guidance contained in Waste Management Paper No. 26 (DoE, 1986). These sites were rarely capped, tended to have minimal soil cover and had little or no provision for leachate and gas control. Attempts at woodland establishment on such sites have, not infrequently, resulted in substantial tree mortality and sometimes outright failure. Failure has often been blamed on toxicity of wastes, landfill gas, leachate and excessive soil temperatures (e.g. Gawn, 1991; Wilson, 1991), and this has led to a widely held belief that trees cannot be successfully grown on landfill sites (e.g. DoE, 1986). In some instances, contamination of soils with landfill gas has undoubtedly played a large part in the poor performance of trees (Leone *et al.*, 1979; Gilman *et al.*, 1985). However, the evidence for a role of toxic wastes, high temperatures and leachate in widespread tree mortality is more ambiguous (Moffat and Houston, 1991, Wilson, 1991). Too often, these factors appear to be used as an excuse for stunted and dying trees when the underlying cause(s) may have more to do with inadequate site restoration and contouring, poor silvicultural practice, and a lack of proper tree maintenance (cf. Gilman *et al.*, 1982). Examination of tree growth on 19 landfill sites in England during the summer of 1991, as part of this review (Table 2.1 and Appendix 1), revealed that tree performance was extremely variable. When high standards of restoration and silvicultural practice were achieved, tree growth was good, and in some cases excellent (Plates 6, 7 and front cover), but where standards were low, tree growth was stunted and there were high levels of tree mortality.

2.2 It is clear from Table 2.1 that trees can grow well on some landfill sites. It is also clear that poor growth is equally common. In order to understand why some tree planting schemes succeed and others fail it is necessary to establish cause-effect relationships. It is thus important to identify the factors responsible for poor growth, and their relative importance, because only then will it be possible to devise restoration strategies which enable woodland to be successfully established on landfill sites.

Table 2.1 Frequency of planting and performance of trees on 19 landfill sites in the UK (tree age in the range of approximately 5–25 years). Scientific names of tree species may be found in Appendix 2.

Species	No. sites	Tree condition		
		Good	Moderate	Poor
Ash	10	3	3	4
English oak	10	3	4	3
Sycamore	9	2	3	4
Birch	8	4	1	3
Italian alder	8	3	4	1
Common alder	7	2	5	0
Grey alder	7	2	3	2
Corsican pine	6	3	1	2
Cherry	5	4	0	1
Field maple	5	1	3	1
Red alder	5	1	2	2
Beech	4	0	0	4
Hornbeam	4	1	1	2
Scots pine	4	2	1	1
Swedish whitebeam	4	2	1	1
Willow	4	1	2	1

Landfill gas

Composition and effects on trees and soil

2.3 Landfill gas is the complex mixture of gases formed during the decomposition of biodegradable wastes in a landfill site. A typical landfill gas comprises about 64% methane and 34% carbon dioxide, plus trace concentrations of a range of organic gases and vapours (Table 2.2). These gases escape along paths of least resistance, either through the top surface, or by diffusion through permeable strata bordering the site, or, if both the top and sides are impermeable, through cracks that may be present in sealing materials (Wilson, 1985). Migration of these gases into the rooting zone of vegetation growing on top of restored landfills has often caused plant death (Leone *et al.*, 1977; Flower *et al.*, 1981). On sites with no cap and no gas control systems, landfill gas may vent across the whole restoration surface, although the dynamic nature of gas production frequently results in localised 'hot spots' typified by patches of dead or dying vegetation (Moffat and Houston, 1991; Plate 8). Unlined landfilled sand and gravel pits and hard rock quarries can be particularly prone to lateral gas migration, and in the USA death of vegetation has been recorded up to 200 m from the edge of a landfill where such migration has occurred (Flower *et al.*, 1981).

2.4 In modern landfills which tend to be manipulated to enhance gas production (Leach and Moss, 1989), either to speed up the stabilisation of the landfill, or for energy generation, it might be expected that problems from landfill gas would increase. However, with the development of gas management schemes and improved standards of cap design and engineering this has not been the case. Localised areas of dead vegetation associated with fissures or weaknesses in the cap are not uncommon, but extensive dieback visually affecting the overall restoration is rare (Wilson, 1991). Most incidences of widespread dieback have occurred when landfill gas has been allowed to escape, uncontrolled, into cover soils.

2.5 The harmful effect of landfill gas lies primarily, but not exclusively, in its ability to physically displace oxygen from the soil atmosphere (Flower *et al.*, 1981). Exclusion of

Table 2.2 Typical landfill gas composition.

Component	Typical value (% volume)	Observed maximum (%volume)
Methane	63.8	88.0
Carbon dioxide	33.6	89.3
Oxygen	0.16	20.9
Nitrogen	2.4	87.0
Hydrogen	0.05	21.1
Carbon monoxide	0.001	0.0
Ethane	0.005	0.0139
Ethene (ethylene)	0.018	-
Acetaldehyde	0.005	-
Propane	0.002	0.0171
Butane	0.003	0.023
Helium	0.00005	-
Higher alkanes	<0.05	0.07
Unsaturated hydrocarbons	0.009	0.048
Halogenated compounds	0.00002	0.032
Hydrogen sulphide	0.00002	35.0
Organosulphur compounds	0.00001	0.028
Alcohols	0.00001	0.127
Others	0.00005	0.023

Taken from Waste Management Paper No. 27 (DoE, 1991b)

oxygen eventually results in the development of an anaerobic soil, which is then unable to sustain plant growth (see Chapter 3). Methane which usually constitutes the largest proportion, by volume, of landfill gas is not considered to be toxic to plants *per se* (Pankhurst, 1980). However, it may act as a food source for methanogenic bacteria which consume oxygen in the process of breaking down (oxidising) methane to form carbon dioxide and water (Hoeks, 1983):

$$CH_4 + 2O_2 \longrightarrow CO_2 + 2H_2O$$

The degree of oxygen depletion depends on the gas production rate, the depth of soil cover, and the porosity of the soil (Flower *et al.*, 1981). Figure 2.1 represents the gas composition of soil cover (not underlain by a low permeability cap) where the oxidation capacity exceeds the methane production rate (Hoeks, 1983). At increasing methane production rates the depth of the oxidation zone decreases and ultimately methane reaches the soil surface and escapes into the atmosphere. The maximum depth of the oxidation zone is often visually identifiable by a grey/green front in the soil profile (Plate 9).

2.6 In contrast to methane, elevated levels of carbon dioxide have been shown to be toxic to plant roots (see Chapter 3). Its damaging effects are accentuated when oxygen levels are low (Leone *et al.*, 1979). Growth inhibition caused by carbon dioxide varies between species; some are affected at concentrations as low as 1% whilst others are unaffected at 20% (Arthur *et al.*, 1981).

2.7 Trees affected by landfill gas typically exhibit wilting and yellowing of the leaves, premature leaf loss and stunted growth of roots and shoots. Severely affected trees die.

Minor constituents of landfill gas

2.8 Although the principal damaging effects of landfill gas are mediated through the development of anaerobic soil conditions, some

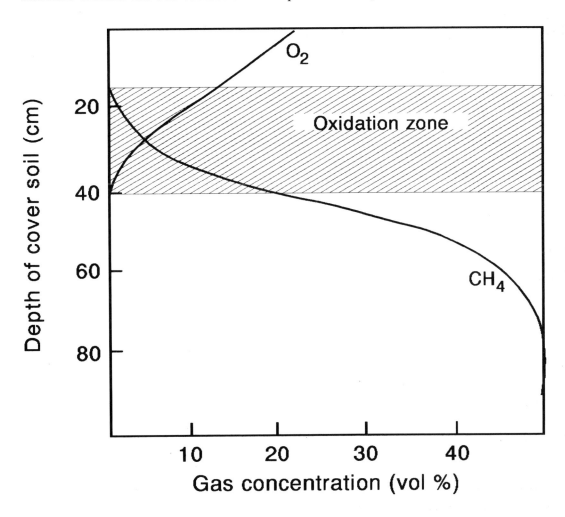

Figure 2.1 Schematic diagram to illustrate gas composition in landfill cover soil (in the absence of a low permeability cap), as influenced by methane oxidation (reprinted from Hoeks, 1983, by permission of Academic Press Inc.).

trace gases can also be important causes of injury.

Ethylene

2.9 Ethylene (ethene) is typically present in landfill gas at concentrations of about 180 ppm. It also occurs naturally in plants in very low concentrations, acting as a growth hormone. Excess concentrations can thus interfere with the hormonal control of growth. Threshold concentrations of ethylene known to disturb plant growth in the laboratory are in the range of approximately 1–5 ppm (Jacobson and Clyde-Hill, 1970). The primary effect of ethylene on roots appears to be root deformation and inhibition of root extension. For example, Crossett and Campbell (1975) found that exposure of barley roots to 10 ppm ethylene retarded the extension of root tips whilst stimulating the growth of lateral roots. In addition, exposure to ethylene appears to favour the growth of shoots at the expense of roots (Scott-Russell, 1977). A possible consequence of this could be increased susceptibility to drought, if the reduced root system is unable to supply the evaporative needs of the shoot.

2.10 Exposure of the shoots to high concentrations of ethylene results in injury similar to that produced by plant hormone-type herbicides (Tattar, 1978) e.g. growth reduction, leaf and bud abscission, leaf yellowing and necrosis, and epinasty (the downward curvature of a plant organ, usually leaves, as a result of more rapid growth on its upper side). It also causes a general growth reduction, stimulation of lateral growth and a decrease of apical dominance.

Hydrogen sulphide

2.11 Hydrogen sulphide is another minor constituent of landfill gas which can be toxic to plants in small concentrations (Scott-Russell, 1977). A typical concentration in landfill gas is 0.2 ppm, but levels of up to 35% by volume have been recorded (DoE, 1991b). In fumigation experiments, effects on plants have rarely been found below a concentration of 400 ppm (Jacobsen and Clyde-Hill, 1970). Hence, only in exceptional circumstances, e.g. where the presence of large quantities of plasterboard (containing calcium sulphate) in the waste may enhance production of hydrogen sulphide, will injury be expected. If large quantities of ferrous iron are present in the soil, hydrogen sulphide

may be rendered non-toxic through the formation of highly insoluble iron sulphide.

Other gases

2.12 A number of other components of landfill gas, including ammonia, hydrogen, mercaptans and butyric acid, have been reported as toxic to trees (Leone et al., 1977), but data on their effects are generally lacking.

Tolerance to landfill gas

2.13 Attempts to identify tree species that are tolerant to landfill gas have met with limited success. The hypothesis that trees which tolerate waterlogging may also be able to tolerate exposure to landfill gas was tested by Arthur et al. (1981). They found that red maple (tolerant of waterlogging) grew better when its roots were exposed to simulated landfill gas than sugar maple (intolerant of waterlogging). However, both species were in noticeably worse condition than control trees treated with ambient air. The red maple, despite being relatively more tolerant than sugar maple, exhibited significant signs of stress (chlorosis and abscission of leaves), and failed to produce any adventitious roots, the usual adaptation to flooding. Leone et al. (1982) tested 19 tree species for tolerance to landfill gas and found that honey locust and green ash (tolerant to poor soil aeration) were amongst the least tolerant trees to landfill gas. It appears from a further description of this work (Gilman et al., 1981) that the most tolerant of the species tested (Japanese black pine and Norway spruce) were only able to tolerate landfill gas because their root systems were shallow enough (<10 cm deep) to avoid the highest concentrations of gas. Flower et al. (1981) also reported details of this experiment and showed that six of the seven most tolerant species had physically smaller root systems at the time of planting. They therefore suggested that small trees survived better by being able to adapt their root systems to the adverse soil conditions by developing roots close to the surface. Roots of larger trees started off deeper in the soil and were killed by landfill gases before they could grow towards the surface.

2.14 It would appear that a tree's ability to withstand the effects of landfill gas has less to do with its ability to *tolerate* high concentrations, than the ability of *avoiding* anaerobic soil through the development of a shallow root system. A shallow (<20 cm) root system is not a desirable feature in a tree, even on a landfill site, as it will predispose the tree to drought stress and windthrow. It would seem, therefore, that the selection of tree species tolerant of landfill gas is an inappropriate solution to the problem of landfill gas. Rather, the presence of landfill gas in the root zone is something to avoid by good engineering practice (Moffat, 1991).

Excluding landfill gases from the root zone

2.15 If tree planting is desired as part of the restoration of a landfill site, measures must be taken to ensure that landfill gas is excluded from the root zone. Injury to vegetation can effectively be prevented with a low permeability cap in combination with a gas extraction system (Hoeks, 1983). Thus, sites which are engineered to the standards laid out in Waste Management Paper No. 26 and 27 (DoE, 1986; 1991b) should have no, or at worst localised, damage from landfill gas. Woodland establishment is therefore only likely to be constrained by landfill gas on older sites with no provision for gas control.

Leachate

2.16 Vegetation problems associated with leachate usually only occur at the surface of a restored landfill. 'Leachate breakout', as it is termed, is caused by high leachate levels within the waste resulting from uncontrolled ingress of water into the site, or a perched leachate table caused by relatively impermeable layers within the waste (Wilson, 1991). Leachate escapes through weaknesses in the cap, or on uncapped sites, directly through covering soils, usually at the edge of the site. If the breakout is associated with subsidence then ponding of leachate may occur. However, more commonly, leachate seepage appears as an orange-red or black stained area which can be surrounded by dead or dying vegetation. It is possible that injury to trees results from leachate toxicity (see Chapter 5), but it is more probable that waterlogging and consequent soil anaerobism (Chapter 3) are the main causes of death.

Elevated temperature

2.17 Elevated temperatures are usually a feature of landfill sites; temperatures of up to 60°C have been recorded within degrading waste, although 30–40°C seems more typical (Christensen and Kjeldsen, 1989). Soil temperatures in excess of 40°C have been recorded on sites where cover is thin (Moffat and Houston, 1991). However, temperature at the soil surface is strongly dependent on depth of soil cover, and Moffat and Houston (1991) have shown that temperature can be significantly attenuated with the provision of a suitable thickness of soil.

2.18 It has been suggested that high temperatures will be detrimental to tree growth (Wilson, 1991), and may contribute to accelerated soil drying (Binns and Fourt, 1983). However, it seems that under some circumstances quite the reverse is true. Moffat and Houston (1991) found that at Pitsea landfill in Essex, soil moisture increased rather than decreased with temperature. The relatively high moisture content of the soil cover was explained by upward movement of water from within the landfill across a temperature gradient (cf. Ruark et al., 1983). Warm soils may also favour early spring growth, extend the growing season, and could provide some protection from winter or spring frosts (Ruark et al., 1982). Shoulders and Ralston (1975) found that nutrient (especially nitrogen, phosphorus, potassium, magnesium and calcium) and water uptake of slash pine was improved by up to 50% as temperature increased from 16°C to 28°C. Similarly, Ruark et al. (1982) reported that, as a general rule, increasing soil temperature stimulates phosphorus uptake by trees.

2.19 Root-zone temperatures producing optimum growth of trees lie in the range of approximately 10–30°C, and temperatures at which root growth declines significantly lie in the range 25–35°C (Lyr and Hoffman, 1967; Ruark et al., 1982), though effects of soil temperature on tree growth are strongly dependent on species. For example, false acacia can withstand root-zone temperatures of 40°C with little or no effect (Graves et al., 1991), but Scots pine may be inhibited at temperatures as low as 25°C. It nevertheless seems unlikely that soil temperatures found on modern landfill sites will be much above ambient where the engineered cap consists of a metre or more of compacted clay. Thus, although some modifications of tree root activity and growth may occur, tree death is unlikely. In situations where temperatures exceed about 30°C, tree damage may have more to do with soil anaerobism, than temperature *per se*. This is because high temperatures increase the oxygen requirement of growing root tips (Rajappan and Boynton, 1956) and stimulate the activity of oxygen-consuming soil organisms (Lyr and Hoffman, 1967).

11

Shallow soil

2.20 Waste Management Paper No. 26 (DoE 1986) recommends that for most restoration afteruses a depth of 1 m of soil over the landfill cap should be provided. However, in practice, many sites have had an inadequate depth of soil cover to sustain tree growth. The depth of soil overlying the cap is an important factor in determining the available water capacity. A shallow soil may be prone to waterlogging in winter and desiccation during summer. Shallow soils restrict the growth of tree roots and thus limit water and nutrient uptake, and anchorage (Wilson, 1991). Moffat and Houston (1991) showed that increasing the depth of soil cover from 0.5 m to 1.0 m improved the survival of poplar, willow, false acacia and pine by up to 50% at Pitsea landfill site in Essex. Mean height growth of 8-year-old false acacia was improved from 1.3 m to 2.2 m as thickness of soil cover increased from 0.5 to 1.5 m.

Poor soil quality

2.21 One of the major difficulties in landfill restoration is the availability of soil materials. It is often only when soils are lacking, or are of insufficient quality for agriculture, that restoration to woodland is considered (Moffat, 1991). It is certainly true that trees are less demanding than horticultural or arable crops in their nutrient requirements, but they still require a minimum standard if they are to grow well (see Chapter 6). Frequently trees are expected to grow in 'soil-forming materials' which have a poor structure, lack organic matter or adequate nutrients (especially nitrogen and phosphorus), may be highly acidic (Plate 10) or alkaline, or contain toxic levels of certain elements (e.g. boron in pulverised fuel ash). For example, landfill sites originally worked for clay used in brick-making are often restored using clay-rich materials as soil substitutes, which suffer from waterlogging in winter, pronounced drying and shrinkage in summer, high pH and infertility (Moffat, 1991). On the other hand, restoration of landfilled sand and gravel workings often involves materials which are stony, acidic, infertile, and prone to drought. Such materials may be an adequate substrate for tree growth if they are ameliorated and fertilised, but trees can often have a stunted and sickly appearance.

Poor soil structure

2.22 Good soil structure is essential for good tree growth. A soil having this quality provides sufficient coarse pores to facilitate soil aeration, the downward drainage of excess water, and exploitation by tree roots, but also has sufficient fine pores to retain water (Reeve, 1991). However, structure of a soil is also one of its most vulnerable properties. It can be almost completely destroyed by soil storage and the mechanised earth moving often associated with excavation and land restoration. The living components of the soil, such as worms, fungi etc, which are important in developing and maintaining soil structure and fertility tend to be the first to suffer in the process of soil moving (Reeve, 1991). Compaction and smearing frequently occur during soil handling, especially if machinery passes over soils when they are too wet (Gawn, 1991). Earthscrapers are often used for soil handling, and although efficient, they tend to exert large ground pressures and can cause extreme soil compaction (Wilson, 1985). Compaction is probably the biggest single factor responsible for poor tree growth on landfill sites (see Chapter 3). This is because it is directly responsible for reducing pore space, aeration, water holding capacity, gaseous exchange and root penetration (Moffat, 1991). It is thus one of the main causes of stress to trees through waterlogging, drought and poor soil oxygen content (Greacen and Sands, 1980).

Waterlogging

2.23 It is not uncommon for soils found on landfill sites to be prone to waterlogging. Compaction is often a major contributory factor, but materials with a heavy texture, such as clays, also inhibit free drainage of water. The problem tends to be worst in high rainfall areas of the north and west, but even in low rainfall areas, sites with inhibited drainage can experience seasonal waterlogging. Poor drainage may be compounded by the presence of a low permeability cap close to the soil surface which can lead to perched water tables being formed. Insufficient slopes to shed surface water, and subsidence leading to ponding, can also be causes of waterlogging (Wilson, 1985).

2.24 Oxygen content of the soil is rapidly depleted in waterlogged soils giving rise to anaerobic conditions (Chapter 3). This results in a reduction of water uptake because the resulting low oxygen and high carbon dioxide levels act together to reduce root permeability (Kozlowski, 1991). The ability of tree roots to absorb nutrients, in particular nitrogen, is also impaired. This usually results in the loss of green colour in the leaves (Shoulders and

Ralston, 1975). Uptake of phosphorus and potassium is similarly reduced in waterlogged soils, and this is partly due to the suppression of mycorrhizae, which have a strong oxygen requirement, and are involved in accelerating the uptake of mineral nutrients (Kozlowski, 1991). In mild or transient cases of waterlogging, effects may be limited to reduced growth. In severe cases the ultimate fate of the tree is death.

Drought

2.25 Shallow soils and compaction play an important role in the occurrence of drought. In shallow soils the total available reservoir of water may be too small to support tree growth in dry weather. In compacted soils, hydraulic conductivity is decreased and the quantity of water retained at high matric potentials is also affected (Taylor and Brar, 1991). Tardieu (1987) (cited by Taylor and Brar, 1991) found that water uptake was reduced in compact soil to almost 50% of that in the uncompacted control, despite the water content being greater in the compacted plots. This is because tree roots have to exert a higher 'suction' to extract water from highly compacted soil with a low matric potential (Wilson, 1985) (Figure 2.2). Compaction also increases surface runoff and

decreases infiltration. Sandy subsoils used as soil-forming materials may be poorly moisture-retentive due to their coarse texture (Ruark et al., 1983) and limited organic matter content. Growth of trees is significantly reduced by drought, and where roots are unable to exploit reserves of moisture in the soil, or moisture supplies become totally exhausted, trees die.

Poor silviculture and tree maintenance

2.26 Poor silvicultural practice and tree maintenance often play an overriding part in the success or failure of woodland schemes on landfill sites. Barbour (1990) conducted a nationwide postal survey of waste regulation authorities, and found that success of tree planting on landfill sites had less to do with site and tree species characteristics than the degree of maintenance, and the selection of suitable planting stock. Site visits by the authors during this study (Appendix 1) confirmed this finding, and highlighted a range of silvicultural and maintenance deficiencies which have resulted in poor success. These include: planting of trees by unqualified and untrained personnel, the use of inappropriate planting stock (i.e. whips and standards where nursery transplants would be more suited to site conditions), and ineffective weed control.

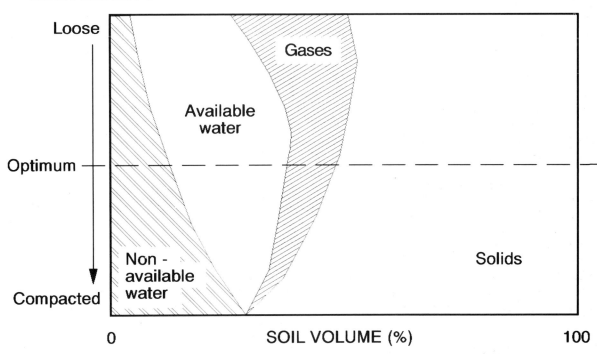

Figure 2.2 Composition of soil at different degrees of compaction (reprinted from Wilson, 1985).

Even on the best sites for conventional forestry, failure to observe basic standards of forestry practice can result in poor survival and stunted tree growth. On the comparatively hostile environment of a landfill site there is an even greater need to observe these standards.

Other problems

Damage from animals

2.27 Trees planted on landfill sites may suffer from animal damage, especially in phased schemes, where complete fencing to keep them out is difficult (Wilson, 1985). Voles, rats, rabbits and hares are most likely to be responsible for damage to trees by gnawing, browsing, or burrowing. Rabbits can cause considerable damage to older trees by removal of the bark at about ground level. Seagulls are also a common problem on landfill sites, and restored areas close to the filling operations may suffer from seagulls pulling up newly planted trees (Gawn, 1991).

Air pollution

2.28 Air pollution may be a problem for trees on some restored landfills which are situated close to heavy industry. For example, emissions of high concentrations of fluorides and sulphur dioxide from brick-making have been identified as detrimentally affecting trees in the Bedfordshire brick-fields (Gilbert, 1983). Clay extraction sites are often landfilled and may thus be extremely close to this source of pollution.

Vandalism

2.29 Many landfill sites are situated on the urban fringe where vandalism can be a problem. Tree planting schemes on man-made sites appear to be especially prone to vandalism, especially where site improvement is conspicuous (Moffat and McNeill, in press). Vandalism usually takes the form of uprooting or snapping of trees, but in some cases has involved deliberately started fires.

Summary and conclusions

2.30 It has been suggested that trees cannot be grown on landfill sites. This is clearly not the case (Table 2.1). On sites which have been restored to a high standard, vigorous tree growth can be achieved (Hayward, 1991). Damage to trees from poor restoration is sometimes due to the peculiar nature of landfill sites, e.g. uncontrolled migration of landfill gas into the root zone, leachate seepage, toxicity of wastes and high temperature. This is especially true of older sites where standards of restoration and pollution control were much lower than those expected of modern sites. However, problems on modern capped sites are more often unrelated to the landfill *per se* but are due to other features of the landfill environment. Thus, many of the problems encountered are not unique to landfill sites, but are common to all man-made sites, e.g. shallow, infertile, poorly structured soils, waterlogging, drought and poor silvicultural practice.

2.31 The constraints to tree growth on landfill sites posed by landfill gas, leachate and elevated temperatures can largely be resolved by good engineering practice, i.e. capping and gas control. Problems associated with planting on reclaimed land, such as compaction and waterlogging, can be minimised using strategies devised for man-made sites in general (Chapter 6; Moffat and McNeill, in press).

2.32 If the establishment of woodland is desired, then the restoration plan must incorporate adequate provision for an environment suitable for tree growth, as this will differ from the requirements of other afteruses (Chapter 6). Amelioration of an inappropriately or badly restored site in no way substitutes for good planning and well executed restoration.

Chapter 3

Rooting habit of trees

Introduction

3.1 It is a commonly held view that the root system of a tree is effectively a mirror image of the above-ground structure of trunk and branches (Figure 3.1a). It is therefore not surprising that the Department of the Environment advised against tree planting on landfill sites with a low permeability cap or membrane (DoE, 1986). However, it must be stressed at the outset that this concept of a tree's root system is a gross misrepresentation. Research spanning many decades (e.g. Büsgen and Münch, 1929; Laitakari, 1929; Laing, 1932; Yeager, 1935; Lutz et al., 1937; Scully, 1942) has revealed that trees growing on undisturbed forest soils typically have a relatively shallow but wide-spreading root system (Figure 3.1b). For example, a study of the root systems of 141 trees by Kochenderfer (1973) revealed that 80-90% of the roots were to be found in the top 0.6 m of soil. Similarly, Lutz et al. (1937) discovered that 96% of the roots of the trees they studied in a white pine forest were located within 0.6 m of the soil surface (Figure 3.2). Perry (1989), after reviewing much of the literature on tree rooting habit, concluded that mature trees typically have 99% of their root biomass situated within the top metre of soil.

3.2 Whilst it is true that in certain circumstances trees can have some roots which penetrate several metres into the soil, this is the exception rather than the rule. Trees tend not to have a deep root system, but rather one which is relatively superficial (Plate 11) but extensive (Figures 3.1b and 3.2). Quite often lateral roots extend outwards from the trunk to a distance of between 1 and 3 times the tree height (Laitakari, 1929; 1935), with the majority of these roots being no deeper than 30 cm (Cheyney, 1932; Lyford and Wilson, 1964). The longest roots are found in trees growing in open ground, but even in dense forest stands tree roots can extend some way beyond the crown projection (Laitakari, 1929). Thus, a good conceptualisation of a tree is that of a wine glass (representing the trunk and crown) standing on a dinner plate (roots). The importance of exploding the myth represented by Figure 3.1a cannot be emphasised enough. Only by so doing will it be possible to realistically evaluate the danger, or otherwise, that tree roots pose to cap integrity.

3.3 The impression that many people have of tree roots is often dominated by the idea of a 'taproot'. The perception that a thick, robust taproot can penetrate deeply into soils, like a biological pile-driver, has undoubtedly contributed to the apprehension expressed in Waste Management Paper No. 26. However, this view, like that described above, is inaccurate; rather, the part of the root system which actually grows into the soil is extremely delicate. Root tips, where new growth is initiated, rarely exceed 2 mm in diameter, and are more commonly less than 1 mm, and constitute a physically insignificant fraction of the total mass of a tree (Romberger, 1963).

3.4 To obtain a correct impression of a tree root system it is important to understand its development, how its final structure is determined, and how developmental processes are influenced by tree species and environment.

Development and architecture of tree roots

Initial development

3.5 The first root to emerge from a tree seed is usually less than 1 mm in diameter, and from it all the other roots grow. Once it emerges from the seed it grows vertically downwards into the soil. This root is often referred to as the primary root, or taproot (Esau, 1953). Initial growth is fairly rapid, so that a depth of between 7.5–12.5 cm can be reached within 1–2 weeks of germination (Sutton, 1980). Lateral (horizontal) roots soon branch from the primary root and proliferate in the top 10 cm of

a

b

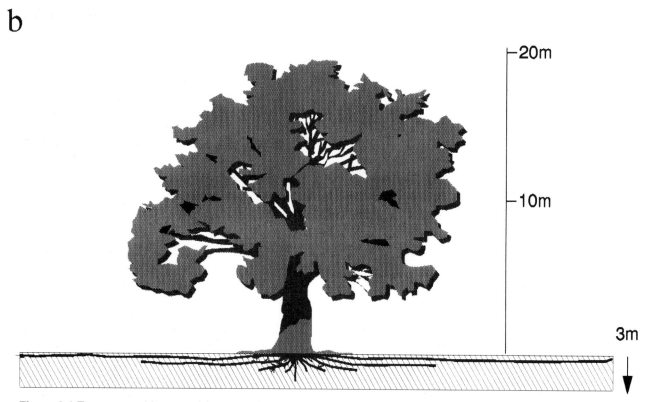

⌐20m

⌐10m

3m

↓

Figure 3.1 Tree root architecture: (a) commonly encountered, inaccurate representation, and (b) more accurate representation (drawn to scale).

16

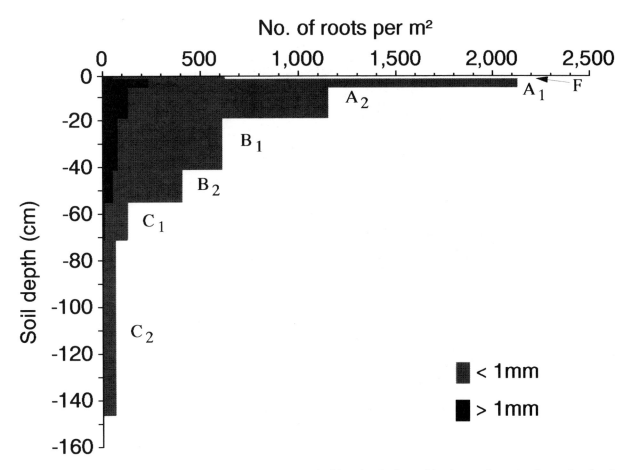

Figure 3.2 Typical distribution of large and small roots of white pine in the soil horizons of a natural woodland soil (sandy loam) (data adapted from Lutz et al., 1937).

soil where water, nutrients and oxygen are most readily available. As the tree matures these lateral roots assume the greatest functional significance by providing stability, acting as conducting vessels for the nutrients and water absorbed by the smaller roots, and acting as storage organs for the products of photosynthesis (Sutton, 1980). At maturity the largest of these roots may be 10–30 cm in diameter nearest the trunk, but they rapidly taper so that at 2–3 m distance they are commonly less than 3 cm in diameter (Lyford and Wilson, 1964). A complex system of smaller roots grows outward and predominantly upward from the larger roots, and these branch four or more times to form fans or mats of thousands of fine non-woody roots (Perry, 1989) which grow almost to the soil surface (Figure 3.2).

3.6 Whilst a vigorous lateral root system is common to all trees, the development of the vertical root system is strongly dependent on tree species, ·environment, and for planted trees, cultural practice (Büsgen and Münch, 1929). In the latter case, nursery grown stock often have their taproot severed by under-cutting or wrenching during transplanting (Williamson and Mason, 1991), though a number of smaller, downwardly directed replacement roots can develop (Bibelriether, 1966). In the past, trees used in the establishment of woodland have been almost exclusively of this type. However, container-grown seedlings now form about 7% of nursery stock, and these may have a reasonably intact taproot at planting (Williamson and Mason, 1991).

Root architecture

3.7 The development of tree root architecture is strongly influenced by species (Toumey, 1929). Contrary to popular belief, only a small proportion of species have a taproot that develops into a major woody root; in many species the dominance of the taproot is lost very early in the development of the root system (Sutton, 1980). In species which have a tendency to retain their taproot form, such as oak, pine and fir (Büsgen and Münch, 1929), the taproot is usually largest immediately beneath the tree trunk but decreases rapidly in diameter as secondary roots branch from it (Perry, 1982). At about 0.5 m depth the taproot tends to have a diameter of less than 5 cm and at 1 m it is generally less than 1 cm (Bibelriether, 1962). The depth attained by a well developed taproot is often no more than 1 m (Sutton, 1969), and in many cases the taproot has already split up into several smaller roots by the time it reaches a depth of between 0.5–1.0 m (Bibelriether, 1966).

3.8 As indicated earlier, the majority of tree species do not have a taproot which persists beyond 5–10 years (Bibelriether, 1966). In species such as spruce, willow, poplar and birch where the taproot is often very poorly developed (Vater, 1927), its main function is as a source of lateral roots (Lyford, 1975).

3.9 For a particular tree the actual form of the root system will depend on the balance of growth between the lateral and vertical roots. Early root research concentrated on this concept in an attempt to determine the characteristic root system of individual tree species (Büsgen and Münch, 1929; Bibelriether, 1966; Röhrig, 1966). It soon became evident, however, that the large amount of variability,

even within a single species, meant that only broad generalisations of root system characteristics could be made. From these generalisations three classic root forms were recognised in the literature; the *heart root*, *taproot* and *surface root* systems (Vater, 1927; Büsgen and Münch, 1929; Kreutzer, 1961; Röhrig, 1966; Köstler *et al.*, 1968; Sutton, 1969). These are illustrated in Figure 3.3 and have been defined by Köstler *et al.* (1968) as follows:

- The *heart root* system, which is characterised by both large and small roots penetrating diagonally from the trunk into the soil in all directions.

- The *taproot* system, with a strong, vertically directed main root starting from the underside of the trunk.

- The *surface root* system, which is characterised by large, horizontal, main lateral roots extending just under the surface, from which a number of large and small roots branch off vertically.

3.10 A classification such as that outlined above is a useful tool for describing general root

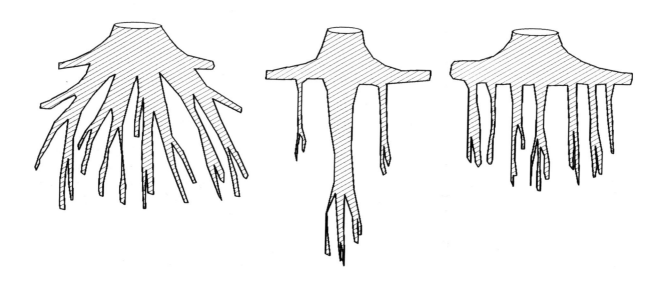

Figure 3.3 Schematic diagram (not to scale) illustrating the three principal types of tree root system. From left to right: heart root, taproot and surface root (reprinted from Köstler *et al.,* 1968).

system characteristics but it should not be used as a rule to rigidly define tree species as belonging to one group or another. Vater (1927) and Büsgen and Münch (1929) warned against this tendency by emphasising that the characters implicit in the three forms of root system are often not retained, and that there are many exceptions to the rule. Despite these warnings, species which commonly have a surface root system, such as spruce and birch, have often been classified as 'shallow-rooted', whilst species which frequently have a taproot, such as oak, fir and pine, have been classed as 'deep-rooted'. Such generalisations are, according to Sutton (1969), *unwarranted and dangerous*'. The reason for this vehemence is that the three categories of root system do not carry with them any implication of intrinsic rooting depth. A surface root system may have vertical roots branching off it which grow to depths equal to or greater than those of a heart root or taproot system (Stout, 1956).

3.11 Bibelriether (1966) demonstrated, through excavation of the root systems of several hundred forest trees, that although genetically inherited characteristics play an important role in determining root distribution, the modifying effects of site and soil conditions are of far greater importance. He found that on favourable sites which had well aerated soils of good texture, all trees developed a more or less characteristic, and relatively deep (up to about 2 m) root system. However, on more difficult sites where soils were compact, stony or waterlogged, the great majority of trees had a relatively shallow root system (less than 1 m). No distinction in depth was evident between taproot, heart root and surface root systems, although these characteristic root types tended to be retained in a 'compressed' form on shallow or compacted soils.

3.12 Many other workers, e.g. Lutz *et al.* (1937), Karizumi (1957), Kreutzer (1961), Röhrig (1966) and Sutton (1969), have found modifications to the 'typical' root system of a species resulting from variations in the soil environment. Laitakari (1929), for example, found that the typical taproot habit of Scots pine was modified by soil conditions to such an extent that a range of different root system types was formed, from a taproot system reaching a maximum depth of 3 m to a surface root system with no taproot and no appreciable vertical roots. He also found that of 25 Norway spruce trees (often thought of as having a surface root system) four had a distinct taproot

(up to 2 m deep), four had a thin, although relatively deep taproot (up to 1.5 m) and one had a stub-like remnant of a taproot. Of the remaining 16, four had noticeable vertical roots and 12 were lacking any vertical roots. Birch, also popularly viewed as shallow rooting was found by Laitakari (1935) rarely to have a taproot but in certain circumstances to have relatively small, vertical roots which were able to penetrate 1.5–2.7 m. However, in water-logged soils, roots were restricted to the top 0.4 m of soil.

3.13 The point of the discussion so far is to illustrate that although differences in root architecture exist between tree species, the final form of a root system is extremely flexible, being determined more by environment than by genetic inheritance (Röhrig, 1966). A further point is that rooting *depth* is unrelated to the structural characteristics of a root system, i.e. whether it is a taproot, heart root or surface root system. Root depth is determined ultimately by the ability of a tree to maintain root growth when the soil conditions are limiting, for example when soils are compact, waterlogged or infertile (Schuster, 1936; Sutton, 1969; Coutts, 1982). Coile (1951) put it succinctly when he said 'depth (of tree roots) is so greatly influenced by the interactions of physical properties of the soil, distribution of effective rainfall, topography, aspect, and the nature of the surface geology, that inherent rooting habit of trees becomes relatively insignificant. Roots will grow in that part of the soil where moisture, aeration, and mechanical properties are favourable.'

3.14 As environment plays such a large part in determining root distribution and growth it is important to examine in detail the different aspects of soil condition which limit root growth. By so doing, it should be possible to evaluate under what conditions tree roots may be a danger to a landfill cap and under what conditions there will be little danger.

Soil conditions and tree root growth

3.15 There are four main components of soil condition which affect tree root development: 1) mechanical resistance, 2) aeration, 3) fertility, and 4) moisture (Sutton, 1969). The most important of these, in terms of restricting vertical root growth, are mechanical resistance and soil aeration, so these are discussed in greater detail.

Mechanical resistance

Resistance to root growth

3.16 Tree roots *cannot* penetrate into soils when mechanical resistance exceeds certain critical limits. Such a resistance can result from excessive stoniness (Laitakari, 1935), extremely fine (Cheyney, 1932) or coarse (Schuster, 1936) sand layers, ironpans (McMinn, 1963) or compact soil layers (Fayle, 1965). Instances where the downward penetration of roots is abruptly terminated at soil layers of high strength or bulk density are legion. For instance, Crossley (1940) found that the taproot of a 21-year-old burr oak on coming into contact with a hard pan split up into 11 different branches. A few of these penetrated a few millimetres into the pan layer, through cracks, but were twisted, flattened and gnarled in appearance. Similarly, a fragipan layer halted the downward growth of Douglas fir taproots (McMinn, 1963). Roots which reach highly compact subsoils and are unable to continue their vertical development tend to deform, branch profusely, and continue laterally along the plane of compaction (Bibelriether, 1962; McMinn, 1963).

3.17 Root growth is reduced in compacted soils. It tends to decrease linearly with increasing bulk density. For example, penetration of soil by roots of Douglas fir seedlings was found to decline linearly with soil bulk density in the range 1.37–1.77 g cm^{-3} (Heilman, 1981). At values of 1.74–1.83 g cm^{-3}, root penetration ceased altogether. Zisa *et al.* (1980) demonstrated that the growth of Austrian pine roots on a silt loam and sandy loam were severely restricted at bulk densities of 1.4 and 1.8 g cm^{-3} respectively (Figure 3.4). For mature Scots pine, Faulkner and Malcolm (1972) determined that root penetration ceased when stone-free bulk density was in the range 1.40–1.67 g cm^{-3}, irrespective of soil type. However, Bowen (1981) examined a range of soil types and found that soil texture influenced the bulk density at which root penetration ceased. Heavier soils were found to restrict root penetration at lower bulk densities than lighter soils. For example, root growth was severely impeded at a bulk density of 1.55 g cm^{-3} on a clay loam, but not until 1.85 g cm^{-3} on a loamy fine sand.

3.18 In clay soils with high bulk densities root penetration is only seen in cleavage planes and old root channels (Foil and Ralston, 1967). Under these circumstances roots can reasonably be regarded not so much as growing *through* the soil as *between* the structural units of which it is composed (Scott-Russell, 1977). Bibelriether (1962) found that for both oaks and firs (tree species with an ability to tolerate some level of soil compaction; Table 3.1) their roots tended not to grow into the clay peds but only in structural fissures and cracks. This therefore suggests that tree roots will be unable to grow into a highly compacted clay cap unless there are pre-existing fractures.

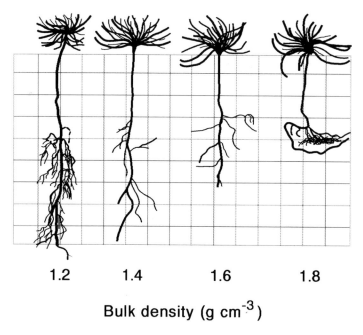

1.2   1.4   1.6   1.8

Bulk density (g cm^{-3})

Figure 3.4 Responses of the roots of Austrian pine seedlings to increasing bulk density in a sandy loam (reprinted from Zisa *et al.,* 1980, by permission of USDA Forest Service).

3.19 There have been few experimental investigations of root penetration into clay caps, and there are none dealing with tree roots. A survey of twenty landfill caps in Wisconsin, USA, was reported by Grefe *et al.* (1987). They found many examples where various grasses were planted in thin (10–30 cm) layers of soil on top of clay caps. Where the clay was found to be loose and poorly compacted, root penetration was extensive. However, where the clay was dense and well compacted, some root penetration often occurred but was very slight, typically extending to a maximum of 5 cm. Although this study was restricted to the behaviour of grass roots, it is unlikely that tree roots would be able to penetrate any further as it seems they cannot exert greater penetrating pressures than other types of vegetation (paragraph 3.23).

3.20 In addition to reducing root elongation and penetration, soil compaction tends to cause growth to shift from vertical roots to lateral roots (McMinn, 1963, Pan and Bassuk, 1985). This is illustrated by the recent work of Bending (1991) who examined the root distribution of 20-year-old Japanese larch growing on coal spoil. On half of the plots examined, the spoil had been loose-tipped, and on the other half the spoil had been compacted and then loosened by deep ripping to 60 cm. In the loose-tipped spoil the bulk density did not exceed 1.6 g cm^{-3}, and roots were roughly evenly distributed in the profile down to a depth of 1.0 m (Figure 3.5). However, in plots that had been compacted and then ripped, almost the same number of roots were concentrated in the top 0.3 m of less compact spoil. The uncultivated spoil at 0.6 m, with a bulk density of 2.0 g cm^{-3}, entirely prevented vertical root penetration.

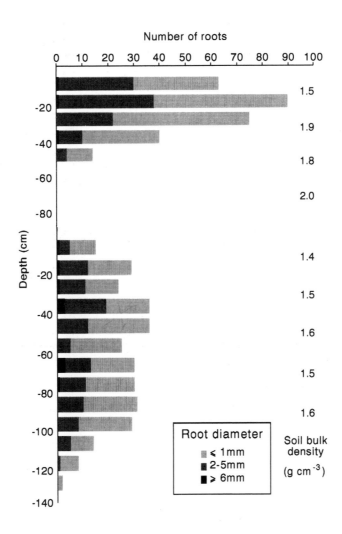

Figure 3.5 Distribution of large and small roots of larch through the profile of compacted coal spoil, ripped to 60 cm (top), and loose-tipped (bottom). Bulk densities are shown for 20 cm intervals (N.A.D. Bending, unpublished data).

3.21 The information described above indicates that the bulk densities required to prevent tree root growth are usually considerably lower than the recommended bulk density of an engineered clay cap (1.8–1.9 g cm^{-3}; DoE, 1986). This strongly suggests that tree roots are unlikely to penetrate a well compacted clay cap complying with the specifications given in Waste Management Paper No. 26 (DoE, 1986).

3.22 Before moving on to examine the other factors which combine with soil compaction to reduce or stop root growth, it is important to understand the reasons why compaction affects growth. When soils are compacted, the particles of the soil are compressed together. This compression increases the mechanical strength of the soil and decreases its volume. The change in volume is brought about by a reduction in the spaces between soil particles – the *pore space*. The largest of the soil pores (macropores), with a diameter of 50–150 µm, are the first to be affected, and it is these pores that are exploited by plant roots (Kozlowski, 1991). Wiersum (1957) has shown that roots in a rigid medium will only pass through pores that exceed the diameter of the root tip (usually >100 µm). Thus, to penetrate a soil with pores smaller than the critical diameter of the root tip, roots must exert force sufficient to move materials from their paths (Taylor and Gardner, 1960). Their ability to do so depends not only on the force they are able to exert (see paragraph 3.23) but also on the compressibility of the medium they are growing into. In soils of moderate to high strength, compressibility is small, and the magnitude of the forces resisting pore enlargement are so great that root extension is either severely restricted or halted altogether.

Root growth pressures

3.23 Roots increase in length because as newly formed cells in the actively growing tissue near the root tip grow, they increase in volume and push the root tip forward. Roots are therefore able to exert a measurable pressure, both axially (forwards) and radially (outwards). The experimental technique for measuring root growth pressures was first described in a lengthy German paper by Pfeffer (1893). The technique he used was summarised in English by Gill and Bolt (1955) in an attempt to stimulate interest in the measurement of root growth pressures. More recently, Gregory

(1988) has reviewed available data, and has shown that maximum root growth pressures of a range of vegetation types were in the range 0.7–2.5 MPa. However, the data included measurements on only one tree species, horse chestnut (0.7 MPa).

3.24 The growth of tree roots has been shown to decrease exponentially as soil strength increases (Greacen and Sands, 1980). Taylor and Ratliff (1969) found that penetration of roots into four soils was reduced by 50% when penetrometer resistance was about 0.7 MPa, by about 80% at 1.4 MPa and effectively ceased at 2.0 MPa. Greacen and Sands (1980) suggested that for most tree species and soil types, the upper limit for root growth was about 2.5 MPa. This value is of a similar magnitude to maximum root growth pressures measured.

3.25 A typical value of the pressure required to puncture or tear a 2.5 mm thick high density polyethylene liner is about 24 MPa. This is approximately ten times greater than the maximum pressure which can be exerted by a tree root.

3.26 Root growth pressures are greatly reduced when soil conditions are unfavourable. For example, reduction in oxygen concentration or temperature around the elongation zone, and soil compaction all reduce root growth pressure (Taylor and Brar, 1991; Greacen, 1986). Anchorage is also necessary for roots to exert their maximum force against the soil matrix. If anchorage is not present, the root tip may remain stationary and growth in the elongation zone will cause spiralling or some other distortion (Taylor and Brar, 1991). Figure 3.6 illustrates how roots are deflected at an interface between a dense medium and a soil of fine or coarse texture. With a fine textured material the root has better anchorage and is able to penetrate the dense substrate below more easily, whereas the root in coarse material has poorer anchorage and is deflected along the surface of the dense medium (Dexter, 1986). The effectiveness of coarse sand and gravel in preventing root penetration into lower soil layers has been recognised by Schuster (1936) amongst many others. This suggests that a layer of coarse material above a fine-textured, dense, clay cap could be useful in the prevention of root penetration, and therefore reinforces the recommendation made by Knox (1991a) that a coarse drainage layer should be placed directly above the cap (see paragraphs 5.2 and 6.22).

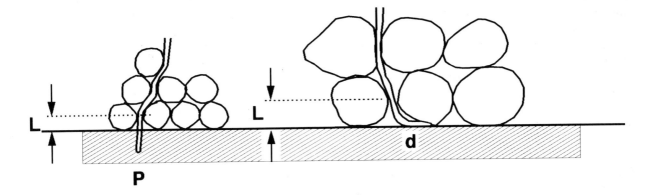

Figure 3.6 The behaviour of a root upon reaching a dense subsoil layer in a fine soil (left) and a coarse soil (right). The fine soil has only small air-gap lengths (**L**), whereas the coarser material has larger air-gap lengths. At the interface between the two layers, small values of **L** give a greater chance of root penetration (**p**) into the dense layer, whereas larger values of **L** increase the likelihood of root deflection (**d**). This is because larger values of **L** lead to root buckling and hence deflection along the interface (reprinted from Dexter, 1986, by permission of Kluwer Academic Publishers).

Aeration

3.27 The roots of virtually all trees commonly planted in Britain are unable to grow in areas of the soil where there is insufficient oxygen available for respiration. In addition, where roots are deprived of oxygen for prolonged periods of time they die. The availability of oxygen in the soil is closely related to soil structure and texture. In compacted soils the air-filled pore space, and consequently the total amount of oxygen available to roots, is small (Chapter 4; Figure 2.2). Richards and Cockcroft (1974) found that when compaction reduced air space to below 15%, tree root growth was inhibited, and when air space dropped to 2%, growth stopped. In addition, disruption of pore continuity hinders the movement of oxygen within the soil.

3.28 Compaction, particularly in fine textured soils, often impedes drainage, and it is the resulting waterlogging that tends to have the greatest effect on root growth. In waterlogged soils, water occupies the previously air-filled pores and thus restricts diffusion of gases into and out of the soil. Poor gas exchange between the soil and the atmosphere causes a depletion of soil oxygen when it is utilised by the respiration of plant roots and soil organisms, and an accumulation of the waste product of respiration, carbon dioxide (Scott-Russell, 1977). Carbon dioxide in high concentrations has been found to be toxic to roots; the principal effect appears to be a decrease in the permeability of roots, which reduces water and nutrient uptake (Ruark *et al.*, 1982). Prolonged waterlogging eventually results in the development of anaerobic conditions, and under such conditions anaerobic bacteria begin to produce gases such as methane, ethylene (Smith and Dowdell, 1974) and other compounds that are also toxic to roots (Kozlowski, 1991).

3.29 As a general rule, oxygen concentrations decrease and carbon dioxide concentrations increase with depth of soil (Yelenosky, 1964). Thus on severely waterlogged soils, roots only grow in the upper aerated layer of soil so that shallow root systems develop (Laing, 1932). Laitakari (1935) found that birch roots were unable to survive in waterlogged soils, and under such conditions had a superficial root system penetrating to no more than 0.6 m. He also noted that the taproot habit of Scots pine was suppressed in waterlogged soils, so that a plate-like root system was formed (Laitakari, 1929). Similarly, Röhrig (1966) and Kreutzer (1961) found that Douglas fir, which often has a taproot, had a completely flat root system on pseudogley sites. The conclusion of Yeatman (1955) following an extensive study of tree root development on upland heaths was that tree roots would only freely exploit soil which was sufficiently porous and well aerated.

3.30 In addition to inhibiting the growth of new roots, waterlogging can lead to death and decay of a large proportion of the existing root system (Coutts, 1982), often as a result of

23

increased activity of *Phytophthora* decay fungi, which can tolerate low oxygen concentrations, and are stimulated by low tree vigour (Kozlowski, 1991).

3.31 The minimum concentrations of oxygen required for tree root growth have not been clearly defined. However, from the information available it appears that when oxygen content of the soil drops below 10%, root growth is greatly restricted and at about 3–5% root growth ceases altogether (Kozlowski, 1991). The roots of some tree species, however, can survive for a limited period when soil oxygen concentrations are as low as 0.1–0.3%, but at these levels new root growth cannot take place. Root growth may be restricted at much higher oxygen concentrations if soils are compact as well as waterlogged. It is well known that low oxygen and soil compaction interact, so that the effects of low oxygen are greater at higher bulk densities, and the effects of high bulk density are greater at low oxygen concentrations.

3.32 Some tree roots will withstand low oxygen levels during their winter dormant period because their respiration rate is very low, but the same tree during active growth may rapidly succumb to injury if oxygen concentrations remain small (Yelenosky, 1964). Some tree species have the ability to transport small quantities of O_2 from the stem to the roots, e.g. willows, poplars and alders, but even with this ability, survival of these trees can be severely reduced in permanently waterlogged soils (Kozlowski, 1986).

3.33 If data were available on typical oxygen concentrations in a clay cap on a landfill site, it would be possible from the information outlined above to evaluate whether tree roots would be able to grow into it. Whilst specific data for landfill sites are lacking, data obtained by Yelenosky (1964) on the gas composition of a heavily compacted clay soil may be used to estimate oxygen concentrations that might be expected in a clay cap. He found that oxygen concentrations were less than 2% and carbon dioxide concentrations were as high as 20%. Given that tree root growth stops at an oxygen concentration of 3–5% (Kozlowski, 1991) it seems highly improbable that tree roots will be able to penetrate into a landfill cap that is engineered to achieve a high level of compaction. In addition, the gaseous composition of a clay cap will be further altered by slow upward diffusion of landfill gases from below. Clearly there will be a gradient of

methane, carbon dioxide and oxygen within the cap, with anaerobic conditions being especially prevalent at its base. Thus, it is almost certain that even if tree roots were to penetrate the upper surface of the cap, they would be unable to extend far into it as they would be killed by the upwardly migrating phytotoxic gases.

Fertility

3.34 Tree root growth and development are also influenced by soil fertility. Fertile soil encourages the growth of shoots relative to the growth of roots, and increases root branchiness. Roots proliferate in areas of the soil which are rich in nutrients, especially nitrogen and phosphorus, and as nutrients are concentrated in the upper, organic-rich soil layers, so are the majority of absorbing roots (Laitakari, 1935). Long slender roots tend to be produced when soils are deficient in nitrogen, but shorter, well branched roots are formed when nitrogen supply is good (Sutton, 1969). While unequivocal evidence is lacking, it often seems that the less fertile the site, the shallower roots grow. For example, Yeatman (1955) examined tree root distribution on upland heaths and discovered that rooting was shallower on the least fertile sites. Shallow rooting of spruce on infertile sands was also reported by Bannan (1940), and in his examination of tree rooting habit, Laitakari (1927) observed that the shallowest root systems were to be found on infertile sandy soils. In general, soils with low fertility produce root systems characterised by long, poorly branched surface roots, whereas sites with higher fertility produce more vigorous root systems that are well branched and descend deeper into the soil (Sutton, 1969).

Moisture

3.35 Both excess of water, and water deficit, can affect the growth of tree roots. Waterlogging usually results in the formation of shallow root systems (paragraph 3.29), and in many cases, so does drought (Zahner, 1968). It is often assumed that the response of trees to drought is to produce a deeper root system so that deeper reserves of moisture can be tapped. However, whilst deeper roots are clearly of significance during periods of soil moisture deficit, the relationship between root growth and moisture availability is not simple. For example, Bannan (1940) found that the roots of several coniferous tree species growing on dry sand were shallow and plate-like, being no deeper than the root systems of trees growing on waterlogged sites. Similar relationships between the extent of root systems and the extremes of soil moisture have been found in other field studies, with sparse, shallow root development on excessively wet or dry sites (e.g. Cheyney, 1932; Laitakari, 1935; Zahner, 1968). Some studies have emphasised the fact that soil strength increases sharply as the soil dries, and have suggested that the failure of roots to grow into dry soils is therefore probably more the result of physical resistance rather than water stress *per se* (Zahner, 1968). In addition, Coile (1937) and Harley (1940) have suggested that the shallow, but wide-spreading root systems characteristic of some trees growing on dry soils is an adaptive strategy which enables the efficient interception of moisture from intermittent, light rain showers.

Rooting depths of different tree species

3.36 There appear from the literature to be no significant differences between tree species in potential rooting depth on well aerated, loose soils (Bibelriether, 1966). Differences in actual root depth are determined by the relative ability of different tree species to tolerate unfavourable soil conditions. For example,

Minore *et al.* (1969) found that the roots of lodgepole pine, Douglas fir, red alder and Pacific silver fir were able to penetrate into a compact sandy loam soil, whereas sitka spruce, western hemlock and western red cedar were unable to do so. Similarly, Leyton (1956) tested three species for tolerance to oxygen deficit and found that willow was best able to tolerate conditions of low oxygen whereas Scots pine was less able and Norway spruce least able. Shallow rooting can thus be the consequence of a number of different factors, such as soil compaction, or poor soil aeration, acting either separately or together.

3.37 Data comparing root growth on a similar soil type is necessary to determine genetic differences in rooting habit between tree species. Comparative data for a number of European forest tree species are available from Bibelriether (1966) and Köstler *et al.* (1968), and these are presented in Table 3.1. It is interesting to note that the roots of Scots pine and silver fir (taproot), common alder, Douglas fir and European larch, (heart root) and Norway spruce (surface root) all reach average depths of 2 m on well aerated, sandy soils. However, of these species, only common alder and silver fir showed a degree of tolerance to both soil compaction and poor aeration.

Table 3.1 Characteristics of root systems of mature European broadleaved and coniferous tree species growing on well aerated, sandy soils. Such soils present minimum resistance to root penetration. The ability of roots to penetrate into compact or stony soils, and to tolerate poor soil aeration is also shown. Scientific names of tree species may be found in Appendix 2. (Data adapted from Bibelriether, 1966 and Köstler *et al.,* 1968).

Species	Typical root system architecture	Typical root depth (m)	Mechanical root penetration	Tolerance to O_2 deficit
Ash	Surface root	1.1	Medium	Medium-high
Aspen	Surface root	1.3	High	High
Birch	Heart root	1.8	Medium	Low
Beech	Heart root	1.3	Low	Low
Common alder	Heart/surface root	2.0	High	High
Corsican pine	Taproot	–	Medium	–
Douglas fir	Heart root	2.0	High	Medium-low
English oak	Taproot	1.5	High	High
European larch	Heart root	2.0	High	Medium
Hornbeam	Heart root	1.6	Medium	Medium
Japanese larch	Heart root	–	Medium	Medium
Lime	Heart root	1.3	Low	Low
Norway maple	Heart root	1.0	–	Medium
Norway spruce	Surface root	2.0	Low	Very low
Red oak	Heart root	1.6	Medium	Medium-high
Scots pine	Taproot	2.1	High	Medium
Sessile oak	Taproot	1.5	High	High
Silver fir	Taproot	2.0	High	High
Sycamore	Heart root	1.3	Low	Low
White pine	Surface root	1.7	Low	Very low

3.38 Gasson and Cutler (1990) compiled a large amount of data on the depths of tree root plates after the October 1987 storm in the south of England (Table 3.2). These data give a good guide to the depths achieved by roots of a wide range of tree genera, although it must be borne in mind that fine roots will have been present below the depth of the root plate. It could be argued that the roots of windblown trees are not representative of the general tree population, as it may only have been the shallowest rooting trees that blew down. However, the data gathered in this survey agree well with information from excavated root systems of standing forest trees (paragraphs 3.1–3.4). Due to the fact that only general information was published on the soil conditions associated with these observations, it is difficult to assess the significance of differences in root depth between species. However, as a general indication of rooting depth they are extremely useful. For instance, they indicate that only 2% of the trees recorded had a taproot, that 44% of root plates were no deeper than 1 m, 95% were no deeper than 2 m, and that the deepest root plate was found to be only 3 m deep.

Table 3.2 Summary of data from the Kew Wind Blown Tree Survey (adapted from Gasson and Cutler, 1990) on maximum depths of roots in the root plates of wind blown trees. The number of trees having maximum root plate depths in the categories <0.5 m, 0.5–1.0 m, 1.0–1.5 m, 1.5–2.0 m and >2.0 m are shown. Scientific names of tree genera may be found in Appendix 2.

Genus	Maximum root plate depth (m)					Total number of trees	Range of root plate depths (m)
	<0.5	0.5–1.0	1.0–1.5	1.5–2.0	>2.0		
Apple	1	2	4	0	1	8	0.45–2.70
Ash	0	10	14	4	3	31	0.75–2.80
Beech	5	28	52	14	4	103	0.10–2.80
Birch	4	13	13	1	1	32	0.10–3.00
Cedar	1	1	1	0	0	3	1.00–2.00
Cherry	0	0	3	3	0	6	1.00–1.55
Chestnut	1	6	14	1	2	24	0.20–2.19
Cypress	3	9	2	0	0	14	0.65–1.81
Douglas fir	1	3	1	0	0	5	0.30–1.45
False acacia	3	1	0	0	0	4	1.59–2.00
False cypress	2	3	2	1	0	8	0.85–1.30
Fir	1	4	4	3	2	14	0.25–2.17
Hawthorn	2	1	0	0	0	3	0.40–0.80
Hazel	1	1	0	0	0	2	0.35–0.75
Hickory	1	1	2	0	0	4	0.94–1.94
Holly	1	12	1	0	0	14	0.33–1.00
Honey locust	2	1	1	0	0	4	0.50–1.72
Hornbeam	0	12	7	0	1	20	0.50–2.10
Horse chestnut	0	4	2	0	0	6	0.50–1.40
Indian bean tree	4	1	0	0	0	5	0.62–1.21
Larch	1	8	11	3	1	24	0.30–2.20
Lime	1	6	12	4	3	26	0.12–2.60
Maple	0	15	14	2	0	31	0.50–1.82
Mulberry	1	1	1	0	0	3	0.81–1.50
Oak	4	39	62	31	9	145	0.30–2.05
Pine	2	8	16	5	1	32	0.40–3.00
Plane	2	1	0	0	0	3	0.80–1.00
Poplar	0	2	3	6	2	13	0.80–2.43
Rowan	3	4	3	0	0	10	0.40–1.35
Southern beech	2	1	6	1	0	10	0.33–1.58
Spruce	3	21	10	1	1	46	0.30–2.14
Tulip tree	1	0	1	2	0	4	0.93–2.00
Walnut	1	3	0	0	1	5	0.30–2.14
Willow	2	1	4	0	0	7	0.20–1.22
Yew	4	1	1	0	0	6	0.50–1.70
Others	4	19	6	3	0	32	0.30–1.75
Total number	64	243	273	85	32	697	0.10–3.00
Percentage of total	9	35	39	12	5	100	

3.39 The information presented in this chapter suggests that whilst trees in natural forest soils can have some roots extending to depths of more than 3 m, it is *uncommon* for trees to root to depths greater than 2 m. Thus, although the guidance contained in Waste Management Paper No. 26 (DoE, 1986) that 'trees, especially when self-sown, can have roots extending to depths of 5 m or more' may not be entirely inaccurate it is extremely misleading. Deep root systems are *only* found where soil conditions permit root growth i.e. where soil bulk density, aeration and moisture are not limiting. Thus, on landfill sites where vertical root penetration is limited by the presence of a landfill cap, deep root systems will not develop.

Rooting habit of coppiced trees

3.40 Because trees under the coppice system of woodland management are regularly cut back, it has been suggested that they might have a shallower root system than standard trees. However, there is little evidence available to indicate whether this is true or not. Bédéneau and Auclair (1989a) compared the root systems of a 50-year-old coppiced oak and a similar aged single-stemmed oak. They found that the standard had twice as many roots as the coppiced tree. In addition, the standard had well-developed structural roots whereas the coppiced tree had fewer coarse roots and more fine roots. However, it is difficult to draw any firm conclusions from this study due to the lack of replication. The effect of coppicing on hybrid poplar fine root dynamics was examined by Bédéneau and Auclair (1989b). They found that trees which were coppiced yearly regenerated only one-third the number of roots of trees coppiced on a 3 year rotation. This suggests that trees coppiced at shorter intervals may have a smaller root biomass than trees coppiced at longer intervals. Bédéneau and Pages (1984) showed that new root growth of coppiced birch was severely reduced for several years after coppicing, and that very few new roots developed. Sweet chestnut, on the other hand, developed several new roots at each rotation. Some of the older roots died, whilst others continued their development. Oak appears to respond in the same way as chestnut, developing new roots after coppicing.

3.41 It would thus appear from the available information, that trees managed under the coppice system may indeed have a smaller root biomass than standard trees. However, further work is required to determine whether roots of coppiced trees are also shallower.

Summary and conclusions

3.42 Although under favourable soil conditions trees may develop a more or less characteristic and relatively deep root system, unfavourable conditions in the soil can bring about marked alterations in its form. Thus, tree species that are intolerant of difficult soil conditions tend to have relatively shallow root systems, whilst those which tolerate poor conditions root more deeply. Data accruing from many decades of research on the roots of woodland and forest trees suggest that shallow rather than deep rooting is the norm. It is not uncommon for trees to have root systems which are no deeper than 1 m. Trees having root systems deeper than 2 m are comparatively rare, and it is exceptional for trees to have roots which are 3 m deep or deeper.

3.43 The literature provides a good indication of the soil conditions which prevent vertical root development and promote the formation of shallow root systems. Thus, tree roots are unlikely to grow into clay soils which have a bulk density in the region of 1.55–1.80 g cm^{-3}, an oxygen content of less than 3–5%, and a low level of fertility. It can therefore be concluded from this information that tree roots will be extremely unlikely to grow into an infertile, compacted clay cap with a bulk density of 1.8–1.9 g cm^{-3} (the level of compaction suggested as being necessary to achieve a permeability of 1 x 10^{-7} cm s^{-1}; DoE, 1986) and an oxygen content of about 2%. The concern expressed in Waste Management Paper No. 26 (DoE, 1986) that tree roots will 'almost inevitably' penetrate through capping materials and into deposited waste therefore seems to be unfounded.

3.44 The implications for tree growth on landfill sites are as follows:

• To ensure healthy tree growth, a substrate must be provided for root growth which is well aerated and loose. Soil compaction is probably the single most important factor inhibiting root development, and hence tree growth, on capped landfill sites.

• To ensure maximum protection of a clay cap from tree roots the clay must be compacted to comply with the specifications outlined in Waste Management Paper No. 26 (DoE, 1986), i.e. a bulk density of 1.8–1.9 g cm^{-3}, and should have an oxygen content of less than 3–5%. A coarse textured drainage layer above a clay cap could also help to discourage penetration of roots into the cap (paragraph 3.26). Synthetic capping materials with a high shear strength (such as HDPE) will provide a total barrier to root penetration.

- To ensure that capping systems are not affected by tree roots, a minimum thickness of rootable soil, or soil-forming materials, must be provided above a cap. The thickness required will depend upon the type of soil materials, and cap, choice of species, and summer rainfall, but should always be in excess of 1 m, though depths in excess of 2 m are probably unnecessary (see Chapter 6).

Chapter 4

Windthrow

Introduction

4.1 In its consideration of the place of trees in the restoration of landfill sites, Waste Management Paper No. 26 (DoE, 1986) draws attention to the risk posed to cap integrity by windthrow. Windthrow is the technical term for trees being blown over by strong winds, and it can involve snapping of the trunk or uprooting (Schaetzl et al., 1989). In this discussion the effects of uprooting rather than wind-snap are the issue, because if trees are uprooted the resultant displacement of cover materials bound up in the root plate might lead to exposure of the low permeability cap. Subsequent weathering could result in its performance being reduced. However, despite the logic behind this concern, the planting of trees on landfill sites should not be dismissed out of hand purely because a risk of windthrow exists. The *level of risk* should be evaluated first. If an examination of the factors involved in windthrow reveal that the risk of windthrow is unacceptable then trees should not be planted, but if, on the other hand, the hazard is judged acceptable, then the planting of trees could be considered as an option. In addition, it is important to bear in mind that windthrow does not imply an inevitable exposure of the cap; the amount of soil displaced will depend on the depth of roots in relation to the depth of soil cover.

4.2 Objective methods of assessing the level of risk (or windthrow hazard) for a given site have been developed, and these are outlined below.

Windthrow hazard classification

4.3 Because of recurrent economic losses experienced by the forestry industry resulting from windthrow in conifer plantations, particularly on exposed upland areas in the north and west of the country, the Forestry Commission has developed a system for predicting the occurrence of windthrow, the *Windthrow Hazard Classification* (Miller, 1985; Quine and Reynard, 1990). This classification is designed to enable the prediction of damage likely to occur through normal winter gales, i.e. gales with a mean wind speed of approximately 39 knots (45 mph) and gusts of about 58 knots (67 mph). Winds of this force occur mostly in northern upland areas and often result in annual damage to semi-mature plantations. The classification is useful because it assists forest managers in deciding which silvicultural regimes should be applied to particular forest stands to minimise tree loss through windthrow, whilst maintaining maximum productivity. In the case of landfill sites this system can be used as a predictive tool to designate sites as having a high or low risk of windthrow, thereby assisting in the assessment of whether tree planting is appropriate or not.

4.4 The classification involves assessing four separate site factors (which are known to be closely related to windthrow hazard and can be objectively quantified to some extent), assigning a score to each, and using the total score to allocate one of the six windthrow hazard classes to the forest area. Although this classification was developed from observations of windthrow in spruce stands in the Scottish borders, and is intended for assessing the hazard to conifer stands of at least 500 ha (Miller, 1985), the principles on which it is based may also be usefully applied to assess the potential for windthrow in lowland, broadleaved plantations (Quine, personal communication).

Windiness of the regional climate

4.5 The likelihood of windthrow is not uniform across the country, but varies with a range of climatic, environmental and stand factors. One of these factors, wind strength, is a primary factor in the prediction of windthrow. The north and west of Britain experience strong winds more frequently, and at greater strengths than other parts of the country, and coastal areas are also associated with more frequent gales than inland areas. For the purposes of the Windthrow Hazard Classification a wind zonation map of Great Britain has been produced (Figure 4.1), based on a combination of wind speed data and exposure flag surveys (Miller, 1985; Quine, 1991). A map with a similar pattern has been produced by the Building Research Establishment (BRE, 1989) (Figure 4.2). This shows the distribution of maximum hourly mean wind speeds which are unlikely to be exceeded within a 50 year period (50-year return period wind speed). This indicates, for example, that Oxfordshire has the least windy climate in Britain.

4.6 The score for windiness is obtained by determining the relevant wind zone from Figure 4.1, and then obtaining the corresponding score from Table 4.1.

Table 4.1 Wind zone scores.

Wind zone	A	B	C	D	E	F	G
Score	13.0	11.0	9.5	7.5	2.5	0.5	0

Table reproduced from Miller (1985).

Elevation

4.7 Both mean wind speed and gale frequency increase with elevation, and trees at higher elevations are therefore generally more prone to wind damage than those on lowland sites within any geographical area. Rainfall also tends to increase, leading to wetter soil conditions, which may cause a reduction of root growth and a decrease in soil shear strength.

4.8 Once the elevation above sea level has been determined the relevant score is obtained from Table 4.2.

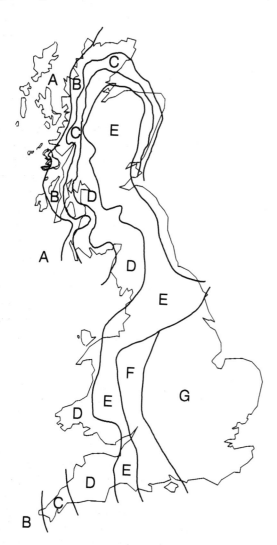

Figure 4.1 Wind zonation map of Great Britain, based on a combination of wind speed data and exposure flag surveys. Wind exposure is graded from high (A) to low (G).

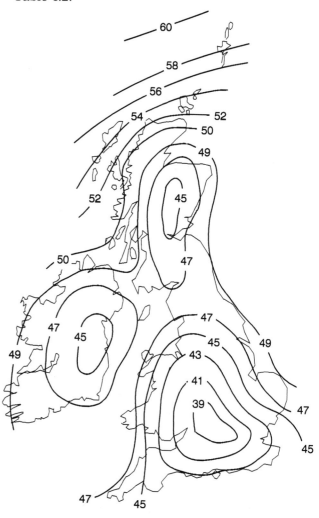

Figure 4.2 Distribution of maximum hourly mean wind speeds (knots) which are unlikely to be exceeded within a 50 year period (50 year return period wind speed). Adapted from BRE (1989) by permission of the Building Research Establishment.

Table 4.2 Elevation scores.

Elevation (m)	Score
541+	10
466–540	9
406–465	8
361–405	7
316–360	6
286–315	5
256–285	4
226–255	3
191–225	2
141–190	1
61–140	0.5
0–60	0

Table reproduced from Miller (1985).

Table 4.3 Topex scores.

Topex (total °)	Score
0–9	10
10–15	9
16–17	8
18–19	7
20–22	6
23–24	5
25–27	4
28–40	3
41–70	2
71–100	1
101+	0

Table reproduced from Miller (1985).

Topography

4.9 The effects of increasing elevation on the wind exposure of a site are modified by the influence of surrounding topography (Hutte, 1968). For example, sites at high elevation may have relatively low wind speeds if they are sheltered by adjacent high ground, and low-lying sites may be relatively exposed if there is no adjacent high ground. The influence of topography on site exposure is complex; the generation of lee slope turbulence, valley funnelling and along-slope acceleration of wind is often of local importance. However, as a general principle it is possible to describe the relative exposure of a site by determining the degree of shelter afforded by adjacent topographic features.

4.10 A simple, objective characterisation of the topographic shelter of a site can be obtained by an assessment of *topex* (Pyatt, 1977). This involves measurement, on site, of the angle of inclination to the horizon at the eight major compass points. As this measurement is land-based, local obstacles such as trees, hedges, etc, are not taken into account. The topex value for the site is obtained by summing together these eight angular measurements. The score relating to this value is obtained from Table 4.3.

Soil conditions and rooting depth

4.11 Uprooting occurs when the lateral forces applied to a tree overcome the root anchorage (Coutts, 1986). The degree to which the tree root system can resist the leverage and overturning forces of the tree stem under wind loading is related to root morphology and soil shear strength as well as to the mass of soil contained within the root plate (Coutts, 1986). As has already been seen (Chapter 3) root morphology is strongly affected by the soil environment, with the depth of structural roots being influenced by soil moisture and aeration as well as the physical nature of the soil materials. Trees growing on wet, gleyed or organic soils are more likely to be uprooted than those on better drained sites, because of shallower rooting, increased incidence of root rots, and a decrease in the shear strength of wet soil. Trees growing on rocky or stony soils also tend to be less windfirm than those growing on stone-free soils (Faulkner and Malcolm, 1972). However, although the depth of the root system is important in determining stability (Fraser, 1962), Bell *et al.* (1991) suggest that it is the lateral roots that often provide the most stability. Thus, for example, Day (1949) cites beech as being relatively wind-stable even on shallow soils because of its wide-spreading root plate.

4.12 The strength of a soil in giving adequate tree anchorage and support comes from adhesive, cohesive and friction properties of the soil (Trousdell *et al.*, 1965). Wetness and saturation greatly reduce soil cohesion and shear strength, thereby increasing the possibility of uprooting. The high incidence of uprooting in the storm of October 1987 in southern England was attributed in part to the exceptional rainfall experienced in the preceding weeks (Grayson, 1989). Work in the United States suggests that uprooting is the major type of damage incurred when hurricane winds are preceded by heavy rains (Croker, 1958), but that when there is little rainfall the damage mostly involves snapped or bent trees (Trousdell *et al.,* 1965).

4.13 Because of the complexity of variation in root architecture and soil physical conditions it was considered necessary within the Windthrow Hazard Classification to adopt a simplified approach, which relates gross root development and soil strength to soil type alone. It is then possible to estimate the relative stability of stands established on different soil types. For the purposes of the classification it was assumed that stability is greatest when soils allow unrestricted root development to a depth of 45 cm or more. Thus, by comparison to many sites used for commercial forestry, landfill sites should provide relatively good root anchorage as they should have a rootable soil depth of at least 1 m.

4.14 An adapted version of the soil score from the Windthrow Hazard Classification is used here which uses two factors, soil moisture and bulk density, to estimate rooting depth. (Table 4.4).

Table 4.4 Soil scores based on root development, and proposed soil groups for man-made sites.

Root development	Soil properties	Score
Unrestricted rooting in excess of 45 cm	Freely draining, non-compact soil (bulk density <1.5 g cm^{-3})	0
Restricted rooting, but some structural root penetration in excess of 25 cm	Seasonally water-logged soil (bulk density 1.5 – 1.7 g cm^{-3})	5
Very restricted rooting, less than 25 cm deep	Waterlogged, compact soil (bulk density >1.7 g cm^{-3})	10

Table adapted from Miller (1985).

Derivation of windthrow hazard class

4.15 The windthrow hazard class of a site is derived from the allocation of a score to each of the four factors described above (Tables 4.1–4.4), and summing of the individual scores. The appropriate windthrow hazard class is then obtained from Table 4.5.

Table 4.5 Windthrow hazard classes (1 = low risk; 6 = high risk).

Windthrow hazard score range	Windthrow hazard class
Up to 8.0	1
8.0–13.5	2
14.0–19.0	3
19.5–24.5	4
25.0–30.0	5
Over 30.5	6

Table reproduced from Miller (1985).

4.16 Each windthrow hazard class is associated with a critical height which is a standard tree height below which windthrow is unlikely to occur (Miller, 1985). The critical heights used in the windthrow hazard classification for unthinned and thinned forest stands are shown in Table 4.6.

Table 4.6 Critical heights for different windthrow hazard classes.

Windthrow hazard class	Critical height (m)	
	Unthinned stands	Thinned stands
1	28.0	25.0
2	25.0	22.0
3	22.0	19.0
4	19.0	16.0
5	16.0	13.0
6	13.0	10.0

Table adapted from Miller (1985).

4.17 It is clear from Table 4.6 that even in the windiest climate, with a windthrow hazard class of 6, windthrow will rarely occur until trees have reached a height of about 10–13 m. In areas with a low windthrow hazard (class 1), windthrow is unlikely to occur until trees have reached a height of about 25–28 m. Table 4.7 shows how tree heights relate to tree age, for sites with productivity comparable to that which might be expected on a landfill site. This indicates that for most species (poplar being the notable exception) trees will be in the region of 20–30 years old by the time they reach even 10 m in height. Woodland trees of less than 10 m are rarely blown over, even in storms of exceptional severity such as that of October 1987 (Quine, personal communica-

Table 4.7 The relationship between height and age for trees growing on soils with a productivity similar to that which might be expected on landfill sites.

Height (m)	Age (y)							
	Scots pine	Corsican pine	Lodgepole pine	European larch	Oak	Beech	Sycamore/Ash/Birch	Poplar
5	22	13	19	11	18	14	10	5
10	36	23	32	23	32	26	19	10
15	56	35	50	38	54	42	33	15
20	92	50	80	63	94	65	72	22
25	-	75	-	-	-	106	-	32
30	-	-	-	-	-	-	-	58

tion). The maximum height achieved by the majority of tree species on landfill sites is likely to be less than 25 m, but those that do reach this height will probably be in the region of 75–100 years old.

4.18 Tree age is relevant to the discussion of windthrow hazard because of the way it relates to the timescale of landfill processes. Whilst the risk of windthrow increases over time, the corresponding potential of landfill sites to cause pollution declines. Precise data are not available but it seems likely that gas production will tail off significantly between 20–40 years after capping (Lawson, personal communication) and that some of the more important components of leachate (such as BOD and COD) will have attenuated considerably during this timespan (Ehrig, 1989). Pollutants such as ammonia and chloride may nevertheless persist in high concentrations for much longer periods of time (Robinson, 1991). However, given the general decline in pollutant concentrations, and depending upon the leachate treatment facilities operating on site, it may be considered that the additional risk posed from windthrow after, for example, 50 years is acceptable.

Catastrophic wind events

4.19 It is evident from the consideration of windthrow hazard above, that the risk of trees blowing over in normal winter gales is very small in most parts of the country, even when trees have reached maturity. However, probably the focus of greatest concern is the occurrence of winds of exceptional severity which can cause *catastrophic windthrow*. Such storms are infrequent, much harder to predict and can result in the devastation of large areas of forest and woodland. However, here again it would be wrong to dismiss tree planting on landfill sites purely because these catastrophic wind events occur. The methodology of risk

assessment (as used by insurers) can also be applied in this case. The usual procedure is to calculate *return periods*, which are a measure of the average time interval between storms of similar force. In the long-term, risk of catastrophic wind events has a similar distribution to normal winter gales, so the wind zonation maps produced by the Forestry Commission (Figure 4.1) and the Building Research Establishment (Figure 4.2) can be usefully applied (Quine, personal communication).

4.20 In the last 45 years catastrophic tree damage has been recorded in this country five times; 1953 in north-east Scotland, 1968 in west Scotland, 1976 in Wales, 1987 in south-east England, and 1990 in south England and south Wales (Quine, 1991). If the most severe of these storms is taken as an example, October 1987, it was estimated that 15 million trees, representing almost 4 million cubic metres of timber (Grayson, 1989), were blown down. This is roughly equal to the total volume of timber windthrown in the other storms put together (Quine, 1991). However, an examination of the return periods involved emphasises the rarity of this event. The mean maximum gusts experienced in this storm were 80 knots (92 mph). In the south-east of England gusts in excess of 80 knots have a return period in excess of 200 years and gusts of 70 knots (80.5 mph) have a return period of greater than 50 years (Quine, 1991). If gust speeds are combined with the occurrence of heavy rainfall (in part responsible for the severity of damage in the 1987 storm) return periods could be much longer. It is also important to note that even in the 1987 storm (as in previous storms) only part of the country was affected by exceptional winds, and that in the area affected only 12% of the total standing volume of timber was windthrown (Grayson, 1989). In the 1990 storm the volume of timber affected was closer to 3% (Quine, 1991).

4.21 It has been suggested that the greater

degree of damage during the 1987 compared with the 1990 storm was due to the fact that many broadleaved trees were still in leaf, and thus presented a greater resistance to the wind. However, Quine (1991) has argued that the greater proportion of damage experienced in the former was more closely related to the intensity of the winds. That is, when gust speeds exceeded 80 knots, the associated level of damage was in the region of 10–30% of the growing stock, but where gust speeds were reduced to 75 knots, less than 5% of the growing stock was affected. It would thus appear that extremely high levels of damage only occur when gust speeds reach 80 knots (Quine, personal communication). The return period for an 80 knot wind at a particular site can be obtained from the Meteorological Office.

4.22 Young trees tend not to be uprooted, even in catastrophic storms. An examination of trees during the summer of 1991 (aged 7–20 years at the time of the 1987 storm) on six landfill sites within the boundaries of the 1987 and 1990 storms, revealed no evidence of windthrow.

Reducing the risk of windthrow

4.23 An obvious way to reduce the risk of windthrow is to harvest trees before they reach a height where they become susceptible to uprooting. However, in conventional forestry this is likely to be impractical and uneconomic. A tree's shape and size influences the forces exerted upon it by the wind, and thus a more appropriate way of reducing windthrow may be to plant trees which will remain relatively small, thus reducing the total crown area exposed to wind. It is nevertheless likely that small trees, even if they do blow down, will tend to disturb proportionally less soil than larger trees. A list of woodland trees which usually have a maximum height of less than 15 m is given in Table 4.8. Traditional silviculture suggests that trees in unthinned stands will be more wind-stable than in thinned stands (Table 4.6).

4.24 As an alternative to the establishment of conventional woodland it may be desirable to manage woodland as coppice. Coppice is a form of woodland management practiced widely in Britain until the First World War, and despite significant decline since then, is still practiced in certain parts of the UK. It involves raising a timber crop from shoots produced from cut stumps (called stools) of the previous crop. Coppicing can usually be repeated many times

and is a useful means of regenerating broad-leaves at short intervals (usually considerably less than 30 years). The cutting back of stems on a regular basis (rotation) keeps the crop small in size and thus ensures that windthrow hazard is minimal. Rotation lengths can be as low as 2–3 years (biomass production) but are typically 12–16 years (Evans, 1984). It would appear that from the point of view of reducing windthrow hazard, coppice could be a useful management option on landfill sites. Short-rotation coppice is considered in more detail in Chapter 5.

Table 4.8 Examples of relatively small trees (usually <15 m at maturity) which may be appropriate for planting on sites with a high windthrow hazard class (see also Table 6.2). Scientific names of tree species may be found in Appendix 2.

Almond leaved willow	Hazel
Aspen	Holly
Balsam poplar	Midland thorn
Bay willow	Purple osier
Bird cherry	Rowan
Caucasian lime	Scots laburnum
Cockspur thorn	Spindle tree
Common osier	Swedish whitebeam
Crab apple	Sweet bay
Field maple	Violet willow
Gean	Whitebeam
Goat willow	White poplar
Grey willow	Yew
Hawthorn	

4.25 There are very few data available to evaluate the stability of different woodland tree species commonly used in the UK. A survey of windblown trees after the 1987 storm, carried out by the Jodrell Laboratory, Royal Botanic Gardens, Kew (Cutler et al., 1990; Cutler, 1991) suggested that maple, ash, and London plane were particularly stable. There were also indications that fir, willow, crab apple, horse chestnut, yew, holly, false acacia, cherry, hawthorn, and laburnum which are commonly planted in the south and east of England, were amongst the more stable trees (Cutler, 1991). A separate survey of windthrown parkland trees was carried out by Gibbs and Greig (1990) who attempted to evaluate in some detail the causes of tree failure. A total of 3,506 trees, both standing and fallen, were surveyed and the results showed that out of these, a total of 978 (27.9%) trees were damaged in some way. Of these, 654 cases (18.7%) involved the failure of the trunk or a major branch and 324 (9.2%) involved uprooting. An analysis of the proportion of trees uprooted compared with the total number of trees surveyed (Table 4.9) gives an idea of the relative susceptibility to uprooting of the most commonly encountered tree species. Ash appears to be the most stable, followed by Norway maple, horse chestnut, London plane, English oak, and sycamore. Least stable appear to be the limes, beech, Turkey oak, and poplar. It must be borne in mind that this classification does not take into account the soil types encountered in the survey which may have played a role in determining the relative order of species.

4.26 As was seen in paragraphs 4.11–4.12, an increase in rooting depth and shear strength of soil will result in an improvement in stability. Shallow rooting was found to be a critical factor in the susceptibility to uprooting during a hurricane (Trousdell *et al.*, 1965); 51% of trees on soils with restricting soil layers were windthrown, but only 7% where rooting was unrestricted. Similarly, Croker (1958) reported that 90% of the longleaf pine trees uprooted by Hurricane Flossy in the United States in 1956 were on soils with shallow clay pans (clay layer less than 60 cm below the surface); these soils occupied only 46% of the study area. Soils with pans well below the soil surface (at least 1.2 m) were encountered in 25% of the study area but only had 3% of windthrown trees. In their survey of windthrown trees in southern England, Gibbs and Greig (1990) used an auger to measure the depth to a soil impediment. They found that 50% of the uprooted trees occurred on sites with a soil depth of less than 40 cm, but that only 35% were windthrown where soils were deeper than 80 cm.

4.27 Soil texture and moisture content appear to have a large impact on tree stability. Trousdell *et al.* (1965) found that hurricane damage in pine forests was significantly greater on soils with a coarse texture than on those with finer texture, and it was most severe where restrictive layers occurred within the soil profile. Besides preventing root penetration, restrictive soil layers impair drainage and thus decrease soil shear strength (Croker, 1958). Cutler (1991) found that coarse textured soils (sands and gravels) were least able to support trees in the 1987 storm, and that wet sandy soils were less able to support trees than wet clay soils. This evidence suggests that coarser textured soils should not be used as soil cover in areas of high windthrow risk.

Summary and conclusions

4.28 Trees growing on landfill sites with at least 1 m of rootable soil cover are probably at no greater risk of windthrow than most forest trees on undisturbed sites. Nevertheless, reasonably objective techniques are available to quantify the potential windthrow hazard at a particular landfill site, and these involve

Table 4.9 Data collected after the 1987 storm on the incidence of uprooting and trunk or branch failures in parkland trees. Ranking is in order from most stable to least stable. Scientific names of tree species may be found in Appendix 2. (Data adapted from Gibbs and Greig, 1990.)

Species	No. of trees	Number of failures affecting:		% of trees uprooted
		Root	Trunk or branch(es)	
Ash	68	0	19	0
Norway maple	132	2	18	1.5
Horse chestnut	411	11	133	2.6
Red horse chestnut	45	2	19	4.4
London plane	230	12	10	5.2
English oak	539	33	208	6.1
Sycamore	185	13	13	7.0
Cedar	125	9	16	7.2
Oak (other spp.)	164	14	43	8.5
Sweet chestnut	104	9	9	8.6
Pine	116	11	8	9.5
Small-leafed lime	104	10	28	9.6
Common lime	532	65	25	12.2
Poplar	76	10	26	13.1
Beech	442	64	60	14.5
Turkey oak	78	16	3	20.5
Large-leafed lime	155	43	16	27.7
Total	3506	324	654	Mean = 9.2%

assessing windiness of the local climate, elevation, topographical exposure and rooting conditions. Further information can be gained on the probability of catastrophic winds occurring by reference to return periods. The risk posed from windthrow should be balanced against the decline of pollutant concentrations within a landfill over time; windthrow hazard is extremely small until trees reach an age of 20–30 years. If a site assessment reveals a low risk of windthrow then tree planting may be considered as an option. If this option is taken up then practical measures should be taken to ensure maximum stability of trees and minimum risk of windthrow.

4.29 The most effective way to improve tree stability is to prevent shallow rooting through the provision of at least 1 m of well drained, non-compact covering soils (see Chapter 6). Some species appear to be more wind-stable than others; ash, Norway maple, horse chestnut, oak and sycamore seem to be the most stable whilst lime, beech, Turkey oak and poplars are least stable. Soil type apparently plays a significant role in determining between-site variability. Evidence suggests that coarse textured or shallow soils afford the least support to trees.

4.30 Other possible options for reducing the risk of windthrow are removing trees before they reach a critical height where they may be more susceptible to windthrow, planting trees which remain relatively small throughout their life, or managing woodland as coppice.

Plate 1 Waste spreading and compaction using a steel-wheeled compactor. Note cell bund and litter fence in background.

Plate 2 Engineered clay cap. The smooth surface of the clay (background) was produced using a vibrating roller.

Plate 3 Improvement of urban landscape by use of woodland in landfill reclamation (Leeds).

Plate 4 Multi-purpose reclamation of landfill site, with strong woodland component (Leeds).

Plate 5 Phased restoration of a large landfill in Buckinghamshire. The trees were planted in 1990 *(see Plate 15)* on a restored part of the site.

Plate 6 Seven-year-old white poplar and ash on a restored landfill in East Sussex.

Plate 7 Maturing mixed woodland on a restored landfill in Befordshire.

Plate 8 Localised death of alder caused by landfill gases.

Plate 9 Tree rooting restricted to upper aerobic soil as a result of landfill gas migration into subsoil (as indicated by grey/green colour).

Plate 10 Gap in woodland caused by inappropriate use of acidic colliery shale as a soil-forming material in landfill restoration.

Plate 11 Rooting pattern of alder on sandy soil. The maximum root depth was 54 cm.

Plate 12 Placement of soil by loose-tipping onto landfill cap.

Plate 13 Suppressed growth of 5-year-old cherry caused by weed competition.

Plate 14 Good growth of 5-year-old cherry resulting from chemical weed control (1 m diameter spot around tree).

Plate 15 Weed control using 1 m square polythene mulch mats.

Plate 16 Useful timber crop growing on a restored landfill site in East Sussex.

Chapter 5

Landfill hydrology

Introduction

5.1 A primary purpose of a capping system is to minimise ingress of water into the landfill, and thereby to minimise leachate production. Waste Management Paper No. 26 (DoE, 1986) recommends that a cap should be constructed of material having a permeability of 1×10^{-7} cm s^{-1} or less. This suggests that percolation through a cap ought to be no greater than about 30 mm per annum. A recent review of landfill cap performance (Knox, 1991a) suggests, however, that this target value is rarely achieved in the UK for clay capping materials. Data from ten studies indicate average annual percolation rates of about 66 mm (range: <10mm to 200 mm). A factor identified as having a major influence on percolation rate was the presence of cracks in the cap. It is well known that stress fractures can be caused by differential settlement of waste, and that desiccation cracks can be formed if the cap is left exposed. It is often assumed that tree roots could also be a cause of cracking either by direct penetration of the clay seal or by desiccation due to moisture extraction. Chapter 3 has suggested that tree roots will not be able to penetrate through synthetic capping materials (e.g. HDPE) and are extremely unlikely to penetrate a well compacted, intact clay cap. However, the potential for tree roots to cause desiccation cracking of buried clays remains to be examined.

5.2 A second finding of Knox's study was that percolation can effectively be reduced by the presence of a drainage layer above the cap. He suggested that 'covering a clay cap with subsoil but without drainage, may prevent desiccation but is more likely to increase percolation. Leaving a clay cap bare will allow greater runoff in the short term, but will almost certainly lead to cracking and greater percolation in the longer term. The optimum solution appears to be to provide a soil cover of adequate depth to prevent the clay from drying out but to ensure that the subsoil is adequately drained. This combination would appear to be able to reduce percolation to less than 20 mm per annum even with a clay whose hydraulic conductivity may be as high as 1×10^{-6} cm s^{-1}.' Maintaining sufficient moisture above a cap to prevent it drying out, but at the same time, removing excess water, are therefore seen as important. Indeed, in some European countries legislation has recently been passed requiring the incorporation of a drainage layer above a landfill cap (see paragraph 6.22).

5.3 Woodland may have an important role to play in maximising drainage of landfill cover soils. This is because woodland which has reached canopy closure has a considerable ability to reduce the amount of rainfall reaching the ground compared with grassland, with the result that soils under trees tend to be drier. The presence of trees on landfill sites could therefore be seen as beneficial rather than detrimental to landfill hydrology, because the amount of water potentially available for percolation into a landfill under woodland will tend to be smaller than that available under grassland.

Shrinkage and cracking of a clay cap

5.4 The perception that tree roots might cause desiccation cracking of a clay cap probably arose from the observation that in exceptionally dry years trees sometimes cause subsidence, and subsequent cracking, of buildings on shrinkable clay soils (Biddle, 1983). This phenomenon is caused by the ability of most clays to change in volume with changes in water content; as they dry they shrink, and as they rewet they swell. However, with respect to the drying effect of trees on a clay cap, it is important to make a distinction between *shrinkage* of clays and actual *cracking*. Shrinkage does not necessarily imply cracking. This is because clays can shrink by a significant amount before cracking occurs, and in a clay cap shrinkage is not important until it results in cracking. Thus, in order to determine whether tree roots can cause desiccation cracking of a clay cap, it is necessary to determine, firstly, to what extent a clay cap can shrink before cracking occurs, and secondly, whether trees are capable of causing this level of shrinkage.

5.5 The *maximum* potential shrinkage that might occur in a well compacted clay cap can be examined using information on the shrinkage behaviour of clay subsoils. Reeve *et al.* (1980) have shown that shrinkage of a range of clay subsoils is strongly correlated with bulk density. They found that the equation:

Total % shrinkage = 81.50 – 42.1 x bulk density

accounted for 75% of the variability in shrinkage of the 19 subsoils they tested. J.M. Hollis (personal communication) established a similar relationship accounting for 57% of variation in shrinkage, where:

Total % shrinkage = 33.54 – 15.0 x bulk density

At a bulk density of 1.8–1.9 g cm^{-3}, the suggested density of a clay cap in the UK (DoE, 1986), the *maximum* shrinkage is therefore likely to be in the region of 1.5–6.5%, and this will only occur if the clay loses *all* its moisture.

5.6 There are two possible pathways for the removal of water from a clay cap by tree roots, 1) direct absorption by roots in contact with the cap, or 2) by upward movement under a moisture gradient if roots in the soil above the cap can exert sufficient soil drying (so-called *capillary rise*). Information in Chapter 3 strongly suggests that tree roots will be unable to penetrate into a compacted clay cap. Nevertheless, there is the potential for moisture removal by tree roots lying on the upper surface of the cap. However, Reeve *et al.* (1973) indicate that the volume of water available for plant uptake in a clay of 1.8 g cm^{-3} bulk density is only about 7–8% of the total soil volume, or about a quarter of the total moisture held in a clay of this density. Hence, the maximum shrinkage values given above will only be partially reached, i.e. shrinkage will be considerably less than the potential 1.5–6.5%.

5.7 Because tree roots cannot dry a clay soil beyond 1.5 MPa (paragraph 5.9), potential extraction of moisture from a clay cap by capillary rise will be limited to about 7–8% of total moisture. However, as water movement from a less permeable layer (the cap) into a more permeable layer (soil cover) is governed by the hydraulic conductivity of the less permeable layer (Warkentin, 1971), the *rate* of water movement will be extremely slow. Thus, it needs to be recognised that the potential shrinkage of a compacted clay cap is very small, and that trees are unlikely to be able to contribute much to shrinkage because of their inability to extract moisture from clays of high bulk density.

5.8 In determining the potential for tree roots to cause cracking of a clay cap it is also necessary to assess how much clays can shrink before they begin to crack. Little or no information exists from field research on this subject, but laboratory studies of clay aggregates and subsoil cores can be used to provide useful information on the shrinkage behaviour of clays. This research has identified four clear shrinkage phases when clays are dried from a very wet condition: 1) *structural shrinkage*; 2) *normal shrinkage*; 3) *residual shrinkage*; and 4) *zero shrinkage* (Haines, 1923; Reeve and Hall, 1978; Yule and Ritchie, 1980; Bronswijk, 1991). These are illustrated in Figure 5.1. The first phase, structural shrinkage, occurs in very wet soils and is associated with removal of water from coarse pores. The loss of water in this phase can be considerable but the changes in volume are usually fairly small. In the normal shrinkage phase, the degree of shrinkage is proportional to the loss of water, but the clay remains fully saturated, i.e. cracking does not occur. During residual shrinkage, the loss of water is greater than the decrease in volume, so air enters the pores of the clay, and at this point cracking does occur. In the zero shrinkage phase, the soil particles reach their most dense configuration and cannot shrink any more.

5.9 It can be seen from experiments on the drying of clays that cracking is not usually expected during the normal shrinkage phase. Reeve and Hall (1978) and Bronswijk (1991) showed, for a number of clayey subsoils, that the residual phase of shrinkage only began when moisture content dropped below about 20–25% and 19% respectively. They also found that the soil moisture tensions associated with these values were in the region of 4.0 MPa. Thus, by implication, this indicates that desiccation cracking only begins when moisture tensions exceed 4.0 MPa. The maximum suc-

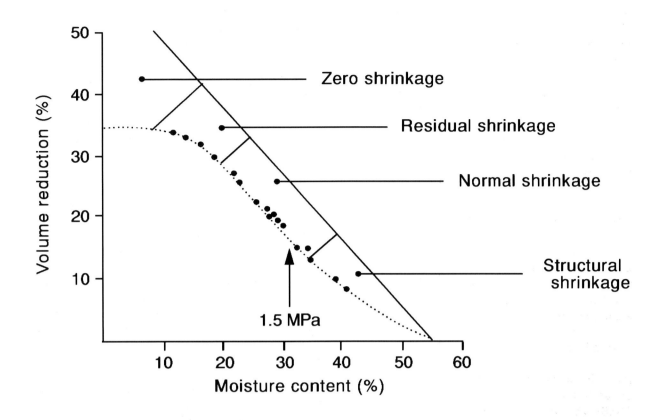

Figure 5.1 Diagram to illustrate the shrinkage phases of a clay subsoil. Note that the permanent wilting point (1.5 MPa) occurs in the phase of normal shrinkage when cracking would not be expected (reprinted from Reeve and Hall, 1978, by permission of Oxford University Press).

tion that tree roots can exert is less than half that of the tension required to cause cracking. Though trees are able to extract water from the soil freely at field capacity (usually taken as 0.01 MPa) their ability to do so declines rapidly as moisture tension rises. Water uptake is severely restricted at tensions as low as 1.0 MPa, and effectively ceases at 1.5 MPa (the *permanent wilting point*; Gregory, 1988). Thus, it would seem that tree roots are unable to extract moisture from clays at the tensions necessary to produce cracking i.e. 4.0 MPa. However, caution must be exercised in the use of laboratory derived data to predict the shrinkage behaviour of a clay cap, and more field derived information on this subject is desirable.

5.10 There is very limited field data on the actual drying of clays which trees can achieve.

The only data available is from monitoring of the patterns of soil drying in the vicinity of isolated trees on clay soils in the south of England (see Biddle, 1983; 1987). Monitoring of soil moisture content (using a neutron probe) beneath a total of 60 trees of 9 species began in 1978 and has continued intermittently until the present day. In each year when measurements were taken, soil moisture was measured twice, once in the spring, when the soils were close to field capacity, and again during September when maximum soil moisture deficits would be expected. The decrease in moisture content during this period was calculated as a percentage reduction of the spring value. Whilst the soils examined in this monitoring programme probably have a completely different structure from the compacted clays found on a landfill site, the results are revealing (Table 5.1).

Table 5.1 Minimum soil moisture content with depth in the vicinity of trees on clay soils. The data are for September/October 1991 following three very dry summers, and are adapted from Biddle (1992). The trees causing soil drying at 3.5 m were all poplars.

Depth (m)	No. trees causing soil drying	% of sample	Estimated minimum soil moisture content (%)
0.5	26	100	30
1.5	21	81	30
2.5	13	50	36
3.5	3	11	38

5.11 Results for the 26 trees still remaining in 1991 (Biddle, 1992), the third successive year of very low rainfall, indicated that soil drying was occurring to a maximum depth of 3.5 m. The maximum reduction in soil moisture content at this depth was 5%. Thus, if it is assumed that the moisture content at field capacity of a clay is 40% (Marshall and Holmes, 1979) then a 5% reduction would result in moisture content being reduced to 38%. Twenty-one trees (81%) were able to cause soil drying to 1.5 m (equivalent to the depth of soil cover recommended in this report for clay capped landfill sites; Chapter 6) causing soil moisture content to be reduced to 30%.

5.12 The information given by Bronswijk (1991) and Reeve and Hall (1978), although not derived from field studies, suggests that moisture content needs to fall below about 19–25% before cracking of clay soils occurs. Biddle's data indicate that trees can cause some drying of natural clay soils to a maximum depth of 3.5 m. Nevertheless, they also indicate that the degree of drying at the soil depth where a clay cap would be encountered on a landfill site (i.e. 1.5 m) is probably insufficient to cause cracking by a fairly large margin (Table 5.1).

5.13 Another factor that may affect the likelihood of desiccation cracking in a clay cap is its shrink-swell potential. High swelling clays with a large shrink-swell potential usually contain the mineral montmorillonite (smectite), which can absorb large amounts of water, and hence are able to shrink considerably on drying (Greene-Kelly, 1974). However, within the range of moisture tensions that water is available to trees (0.01–1.5 MPa), the potential shrinkage differences between clays of different mineralogies are less significant. This is because much of the shrinkage in highly plastic clays occurs at very high tensions. Thus, for example, Reeve et al. (1980) showed that

although there is the potential for a 40% volume reduction in a Fladbury (high shrink potential) subsoil, this is restricted to only 15% within the available water range (i.e. <1.5 MPa). The total potential shrinkage of a Worcester series subsoil (low shrink potential) at 15% is less than half that of the Fladbury soil. However, more than two-thirds of this shrinkage (10–11%) occurs within the available water range. Differences in shrinkage potential between groups of clays are therefore surprisingly small at tensions usually found in British subsoils, with actual shrinkage unlikely to exceed about 15%.

5.14 Whilst the information presented here cannot entirely rule out the possibility that tree roots could cause desiccation cracking in a clay cap, it does indicate that the risk of such cracking is extremely small. This is because compacted clays can only shrink by a limited amount because of their high density, and because tree roots are unable to extract water from clays at moisture tensions that have been associated with cracking. Thus, concerns about the desiccating effects of tree roots on a clay cap seem to have been over-exaggerated. The major cause of cracking in a cap covered by at least 1 m of soil is probably differential settlement (Knox, 1991b).

Water use of woodland

Conventional forest crops

5.15 It is well established that mature upland coniferous woodland has a greater 'water use' than grassland. Many people have taken advantage of the sheltering effect of trees during passing showers, and casual observation reveals that the ground is often drier in woodland than surrounding grassland. The first comparative experimental study in this country was carried out by Law (1956) in a small (0.24 ha) 23-year-old plantation of sitka spruce and an adjacent grassed plot in Yorkshire. He found that water lost by evaporation in the wooded area was almost double that of the grass – a difference of 290 mm per year. Long-term studies by the Institute of Hydrology, in much larger catchments, have confirmed these findings. Over the period 1967–1985, monitoring of water yield at the Plynlimon paired catchments in Wales, showed that the Wye catchment, under grass, evaporated on average 198 mm per annum less than the Severn catchment, under 80% forest cover (Kirby *et al.*, 1991). When a correction is applied for the non-forested area within the Severn catchment, the increase in water-use for the Severn forested area averaged 287 mm, a figure similar to Law's value of 290 mm. Actual evaporation from the grassland was between 15–17% of precipitation, while evaporation from the forested part of the Severn catchment was between 29% and 32% of precipitation.

5.16   There are four possible reasons for increased water use of forests compared to grassland, and these are:

• The lower reflectivity (albedo) of forests (0.10–0.15 for conifers, 0.15–0.20 for broadleaves, and 0.20–0.30 for grass and herbaceous crops; Rutter, 1972). This allows absorption of more incoming radiation, and thus increases the energy available for evaporating moisture.

• The roughness of the forest canopy. This increases wind turbulence resulting in more efficient transfer of water vapour and thus greater evaporation (see Table 5.3).

• The ability of trees to extract moisture from deeper levels of soil. This may enable them to transpire for longer periods during a drought compared to shallower rooted vegetation.

• The ability of trees to retain an appreciable proportion of any one storm (1–2 mm) on the leaves, needles and branches (interception). This intercepted water evaporates without ever reaching the ground.

5.17   Research in Britain has clearly shown that by far the most important of these processes is interception (Kirby *et al.*, 1991). Surprisingly, transpiration of woodland appears to be relatively constant at about 300–350 mm per year irrespective of species,

and is similar to transpiration loss from grassland (Roberts, 1983). By contrast, interception can account for the loss, by evaporation, of between 12 and 62% of annual gross precipittion in upland forests in Britain (Maitland *et al.*, 1990). Kirby *et al.* (1991) reviewed much of the British work on interception and illustrated the potential for large differences between species, with sitka spruce intercepting on average 37.5% of gross precipitation, Norway spruce 34%, Scots pine 47% and larch 20%. Variation between species is thought to be related to canopy capacity, which is the maximum amount of rainfall that can be held in the canopy (Thompson, 1972). Large differences also exist in interception rates between different parts of the country, and this variation has been shown to be related to the amount of annual rainfall and duration of rainfall (Kirby *et al.*, 1991). This is because a significant proportion of rainfall is evaporated from the canopy during the period when rain is falling. Thus, interception losses account for a greater proportion of total evaporation in the wetter north and west of the UK (>2000 mm rainfall per year) because the canopy remains wetter for longer (Calder and Newson, 1979). In the drier south and east where annual rainfall (<600 mm) and duration is less, losses through interception are smaller than through transpiration. This means that the increase in water use by coniferous forest compared to grassland varies across the country from about 15–20% in the north-west to about 5–10% in the southeast (Hall and Roberts, 1989).

5.18   Because broadleaved trees lose their leaves in winter, and conifers retain theirs, broadleaves tend to have lower annual interception rates. Nevertheless, the differences in interception rate between the leafy and leafless periods of broadleaves are surprisingly small. In their review, Hall and Roberts (1989) showed that interception rates for a number of tree species were only decreased by an average of one-third during winter. A suggested reason for this small decrease is that bare twigs and branches, which may be covered with mosses and lichens, are quite efficient at intercepting rainfall, and that during winter the reduced interception surface area is made up for by increased ventilation. Indeed, Norfalaise (1959) found that interception was 50% greater in winter than summer in an oak/birch woodland, a phenomenon which he attributed to the intricate nature of the exposed branches and twigs of the birch. It thus seems that in high rainfall areas the difference in interception rate between conifers and broadleaves is only about 5%, with conifers intercepting about 30% of annual rainfall and broadleaves intercepting about 25% (Binns, 1979). As with conifers, the difference in water use between broadleaves and grass varies across the country, being larger in wetter areas and smaller in drier areas. One recent study suggests that under some circumstances water use of grass may be equal to or slightly greater than broadleaved woodland where annual rainfall is low (Harding *et al.*, 1992).

5.19 The larger water use of trees in most parts of the country results in woodland drying soils for longer, and to greater depths, than grass (Rutter and Fourt, 1965; Biddle, 1987; Hudson, 1988). The presence of woodland on a landfill site could therefore help to reduce water percolation through a clay cap by reducing the total amount of rainfall reaching the soil. The seasonal fluctuations in soil moisture have rarely been compared for grassland and woodland. However, one study by Rutter and Fourt (1965) has yielded very interesting results. Soil moisture was monitored in a Scots pine forest in Hampshire, and a nearby grass covered site (90 m from the nearest tall trees) for 3 years. Over this period (1960–1963) drying of the soils was first detected in April or May. For the forested site the soil moisture deficit persisted until between October and December in 1960, and between February and April in 1963. By contrast, the grass site was completely rewetted in August or September each year. The mean duration of the deficit was 8.8 months for the forest and 3.7 months for the grassland (Table 5.2). This suggests that for the forest, significant percolation was only likely to occur during an average of 3.2 months of the year. Similar results were obtained in the Plynlimon catchment study area (Hudson, 1988).

Table 5.2 Duration of soil moisture deficit under a Scots pine plantation (mean of 4 plots) and grass during the period 1960-1963. Data adapted from Rutter and Fourt (1965).

| | **Duration of soil moisture deficit (months)** | | | |
	1960/1	1961/2	1962/3	Mean
Forest	6.5	9.5	10.3	8.8
Grass	3.5	4.5	3.0	3.7

5.20 Kappeli and Shulin (1988) also carried out a detailed examination of the differences in

hydrological behaviour between trees and grass, by using lysimeters 2.1 m deep adjacent to poplar, alder, Norway spruce, and grass. The annual percolation under grass was found to be 3–4 times greater than that under trees (i.e 480 mm for grass and 120–168 mm for trees). One possible explanation for the large difference in evaporation between trees and grass is that individual trees or small groups of trees tend to use more water than larger areas because they are more exposed to wind and thus transpire more water (Hall and Roberts, 1989). The small size of plantations that may occur on landfill sites, through enhanced evaporation around their edges, could therefore result in relatively greater water use than for larger areas of woodland. The possibility of enhanced evaporation from woodland edges has recently been examined by the Institute of Hydrology at Black Wood in Hampshire (Neal *et al.*, 1991).

5.21 It should be pointed out that most of the work on water use reviewed here relates to semi-mature or mature woodland. Clearly newly planted trees will not have the same water use as mature trees. Nevertheless, water use will increase over time and will be approaching a maximum at the point where canopy closure is reached. The authors have seen an example of an alder/Corsican pine/ cherry mixed woodland on a landfill site restored with loose-tipped soil (see paragraph 6.14) where canopy closure was achieved within 5 years of planting (front cover). However with other tree crops and soil conditions the time from planting to canopy closure could be longer i.e. ten years or more.

Short rotation coppice

5.22 Short rotation coppice is coppice (see paragraph 4.24) having a rotation of less than 10 years (Davies, 1988). The modern concept of short rotation coppice is very like an arable farming crop, but with a cycle of 2–4 years rather than 1 year. Unrooted cuttings, typically of poplar or willow, which are very fast growing, are planted at about 1 m spacing (density of approximately 10 500 stems per ha). After one season of growth, the trees are cut back to ground level. The cut stem resprouts several shoots, and this is the process called 'coppicing'. These shoots are harvested after a further 2–4 years, by which time they may be 2–3 m high. The cut stem resprouts again, and can remain in production for about 30 years before replanting is necessary. The crop can either be used for pulp wood or traditional firewood, but recently there has been a considerable amount of research funded by the Energy Technology Support Unit (e.g. Potter, 1990) examining the potential for using coppice as a renewable energy source for electricity generation.

5.23 The existing information on the water use of short rotation coppice suggests that both transpiration and interception may be significantly greater compared with conventional tree and agricultural crops (Table 5.3). There are several reasons for this:

- Leaf area index is usually larger than for conventional tree and agricultural crops. This means that both interception and transpiration are enhanced.

- Aerodynamic resistance is much lower than for agricultural crops, and thus rate of evaporation is much greater.

- Plantation size is likely to be smaller than for conventional forestry, resulting in a proportionally greater plantation edge. Transpiration is generally greater at the plantation edge because of greater wind turbulence (Neal *et al.*, 1991).

5.24 The available information thus suggests that short rotation coppice could potentially transpire 150–570 mm more water on an annual basis than conventional broadleaf or conifer plantations. Additionally, interception could be 15–35% greater for short rotation coppice than for conventional forestry. An attempt to model changes in water yield upon the establishment of short rotation coppice (Environmental Resources Ltd, 1988) has confirmed the likelihood of a significant reduction in water yield, especially in areas of lower rainfall. Trials established on Finnish landfill sites (Ettala, 1988a and b) showed that short rotation coppice significantly increased transpiration and reduced percolation and leachate production.

Leachate irrigation of trees

5.25 A number of studies have been conducted to examine the potential for disposing of landfill leachate onto tree crops. It has been suggested that the high levels of nutrients within leachate could stimulate tree growth, and that trees and soil could remove potentially harmful pollutants, thus assisting in leachate attenuation (Wong and Leung, 1989). Leachate irrigation experiments have been conducted both on trees adjacent to landfills and trees growing on landfill cover soils.

Table 5.3 Interception, transpiration, leaf area index (LAI) and aerodynamic resistance of short rotation coppice (SRC) compared with broadleaves, conifers and grass (from Moffat, in press).

	SRC	Broadleaves	Conifers	Grass
Interception	30–50%[a]	15–35%[b]	30–35%[b]	10–15%[b]
Transpiration	up to 480 mm[c] (unirrigated) up to 920 mm[c] (irrigated)	320–350 mm[b]	333 mm[d]	n/a
LAI	10 [a], 2, 4, 6–10[c] (unirrigated) 5, 3–14, 7[c] (irrigated)	3, 6–8[b]	1, 2, 8-9[e]	10–15[f]
Aerodynamic resistance (s m^{-1})	10–20[c]	3–10[b]	3–10[b]	40–50[b]

[a] Larsson (1981)
[b] Hall and Roberts (1989)
[c] Ettala (1988a)
[d] Roberts (1983)
[e] Linder (1985)
[f] Sheely and Cooper (1973)

Effects of leachate on tree growth

5.26 The only detailed study in the UK involved irrigation of a coniferous woodland adjacent to a Cornish landfill with approximately 3000 mm per year of relatively low strength leachate (biological oxygen demand (BOD): 10–40 mg l^{-1}; chemical oxygen demand (COD): 50–150 mg l^{-1}; ammonium: 30–120 mg l^{-1}). Irrigation for a period of 12 years had no effect on the visual appearance of the trees (Ankers and Ruegg, 1991). Detailed growth analysis was not carried out.

5.27 In Finland, Ettala (1988b) obtained yields as high as 2.26 tonnes ha^{-1} per year from short rotation coppice stands irrigated with up to 500 mm of leachate per growing season (BOD: 73 mg l^{-1}; COD: 110 mg l^{-1}; ammonium: 120 mg l^{-1}; chloride: 360 mg l^{-1}; electrical conductivity (EC): 0.55 S m^{-1}). Such yields are amongst the greatest recorded in Finland. Injury to trees was not observed, except when leachate high in dissolved salts, particularly sodium and chloride, was sprayed directly onto the foliage rather than the soil. This resulted in extensive necrosis of foliage and premature leaf loss.

5.28 In Ontario, Canada, Cureton et al. (1991) found that irrigation of poplar and willow with a total of 740 mm of leachate (COD: 14 300 mg l^{-1}; chloride 1191 mg l^{-1}; EC: 0.89 S m^{-1}) over two seasons stimulated height growth by 42% and 141% respectively compared with controls irrigated with water. Chlorosis and necrosis of leaves occurred in the second season of irrigation, resulting in early leaf fall, but new buds were initiated after the leachate treatment ended. Gordon et al. (1989), also working in Ontario, found that irrigation of red and sugar maple seedlings with leachate (concentrations of COD and BOD unknown; ammonium: 40 mg l^{-1})

had no significant effect on height growth, but increased stem diameter over a 7 week period. No foliar necrosis was observed. In contrast to the above studies, Menser et al. (1983) working in West Virginia, USA, found that irrigation of six tree species for 4 years with leachate (COD: 1361 mg l^{-1}; EC: 0.19 S m^{-1}) resulted in significant mortality. Survival rate was only 25% of the original planting stock for black locust, sassafras and sourwood. Yellow poplar and red maple performed better with survival rates of 75% and 50% respectively. In Hong Kong, irrigation of acacia with leachate (COD: 613 mg l^{-1}; ammonium: 377 mg l^{-1}; chloride: 992 mg l^{-1}; EC: 0.66 S m^{-1}) resulted in a growth depression of about 25% of the control after 50 days (Wong and Leung, 1989). The trees showed no visible damage.

5.29 The enhanced growth of trees found in some of the studies described above is probably mainly due to increased nitrogen availability. Foliar nutrient concentrations for three studies are presented in Table 5.4, and this indicates consistent increases in nitrogen levels in leachate irrigated trees compared to the controls. The smallest increase was for false acacia (52%) and the largest increase was for poplar (323%). Levels of potassium also increased by an average of 136%, and concentrations of phosphorus increased in false acacia, red maple, tulip tree and acacia, but decreased in poplar and willow. There was little change in foliar magnesium concentra-tions, but calcium content of leaves was reduced by approximately 50% in all the species.

5.30 All the authors were agreed that the reduced growth and stress symptoms found in some of the leachate-treated trees were caused by excessive salinity causing osmotic and ionic stress. The high recorded values of

Table 5.4 Foliar nutrient concentrations (mg g^{-1}) of control (C) and leachate irrigated (L) trees.

| Tree species | Foliar nutrient concentrations (mg g^{-1}) | | | | | | | | | |
| | N | | P | | K | | Mg | | Ca | |
	C	L	C	L	C	L	C	L	C	L
Poplar[1]	9.2	39.0	1.8	1.1	9.5	30.4	7.9	7.8	17.5	10.8
Weeping willow[1]	15.2	25.2	1.5	1.1	5.1	21.2	16.6	9.2	24.6	13.2
False acacia[2]	37.7	57.6	2.6	6.1	15.2	21.8	1.6	2.3	20.7	10.9
Red maple[2]	16.3	47.9	2.9	4.2	8.0	16.8	2.8	2.6	8.4	5.1
Tulip tree[2]	19.1	67.6	1.7	5.6	9.8	23.7	2.6	3.3	16.4	9.9
Acacia[3]	37.5	61.6	1.4	1.9	14.8	11.9	4.6	5.0	–	–

[1] Cureton et al. (1991)
[2] Menser et al. (1983)
[3] Wong and Leung (1989)

electrical conductivity support this hypothesis; EC values of leachate samples were in the range 0.19–0.89 S m^{-1}, and slight to moderate injury to trees might be expected to occur in the range 0.2–0.4 S m^{-1} (Bradshaw and Chadwick, 1980). The high values of foliar chloride (2.0–7.0 mg g^{-1}; Menser et al., 1983; Ettala, 1988b) are also in the range associated with chloride toxicity symptoms i.e. leaf discolouration and premature leaf loss (Dobson, 1991). Taken together, the studies discussed above suggest that, provided electrical conductivity, and particularly chloride concentrations, can be kept at low levels, possibly by dilution or pretreatment, irrigation of trees with leachate should not be detrimental, and could be beneficial, to tree growth. However, leachate used in quantities in excess of evaporative demand could ultimately lead to waterlogging and possibly tree death (Gordon et al., 1989).

5.31 The effects of leachate on soils have not been studied in great detail but it seems likely that long-term irrigation with leachate rich in sodium could lead to a deterioration of soil structure and an imbalance of base cations (Dobson, 1991).

Effect of leachate irrigation on leachate quality

5.32 Only two of the studies described above present results of analysis of leachate quality following application to trees. Ankers and Ruegg (1991) found that low strength leachate applied to a Scots pine plantation was significantly attenuated by the trees and soil so that receiving groundwater or watercourses were unaffected by pollution. Similarly, Menser et al. (1983) found significant improvements in all measured parameters when the leachate treated by application to trees was compared with raw leachate (Table 5.5). Concentrations of the individual constituents in treated leachate were reduced by 75–95% compared with untreated leachate. Overall leachate strength, as indicated by electrical conductivity, was reduced by 90%. These studies suggest that the potential exists for a significant improvement of leachate quality through its use as irrigation water for tree crops.

Summary and conclusions

5.33 At the bulk densities that should be found in a clay cap (upwards of 1.8 g cm^{-3}),

Table 5.5 Chemical composition of raw leachate, and effluent resulting from leachate irrigation of trees (reprinted from Menser et al., 1983).

Parameter (mg l^{-1})	Leachate	Effluent
Ca	186	32
Na	194	37
K	80	7
Mg	62	11
Fe	77	4
Mn	11	2
Al	4.6	1.2
Zn	0.89	0.09
Sr	0.95	0.13
P	0.85	0.35
Cu	0.08	0.01
N	0.04	0.01
Pb	0.02	0.01
Cr	0.04	0.01
Co	0.04	0.01
Cd	0.004	0.001
COD (mg l^{-1})	1878	239
EC (S m^{-1})	0.19	0.02
pH	7.25	6.84

maximum shrinkage is likely to be of the order of 1.5–6.5%, but this will only occur if the clay loses all its moisture. The volume of water available for plant uptake in a clay cap with a bulk density of 1.8 g cm^{-3} is about 7–8% of total soil volume, or about a quarter of the total moisture held in a clay of this density. Hence, shrinkage will be considerably less than the maximum 1.5–6.5%.

5.34 Soil cracking is essentially a surface phenomenon (Mullins, 1991), and tree roots are unlikely to cause desiccation cracking in a clay cap laid to a high standard and protected by at least 1 m of soil. This is because clays only crack when their moisture content drops well below the level at which tree roots are physically capable of extracting water from them.

5.35 Interception and evaporation of rainfall by closed canopy woodland can be up to 20% greater than that of grassland. Thus, if trees were planted on landfill sites, the consequent reduction in total volume of rainfall reaching cover soils under a maturing tree crop could potentially reduce percolation into the cap and leachate generation. The magnitude of this effect will depend on how quickly canopy closure is reached, which is itself determined by site factors, species vigour and tree spacing. Short rotation coppice has a greater water use than conventional broadleaved or coniferous woodland.

5.36 Irrigation of tree crops with leachate has, in some circumstances, significantly improved tree growth and leachate quality. Leachate with a high electrical conductivity (0.2–0.4 S m^{-1}) can cause osmotic or ionic stress and should not be used for irrigation. Stress symptoms which develop as a result of treatment with high strength leachate are similar to those of drought.

Chapter 6

Recommended practices for successful woodland establishment

Introduction

6.1 The information reviewed in this report suggests that woodland can be successfully established on landfill sites, without undue risk to cap integrity, provided that sites are designed, operated and restored to high standards. The report also highlights the need for ensuring the best standards of silvicultural practice and post-planting tree maintenance. A high quality of aftercare is necessary because even if restored well, landfill sites can be comparatively hostile places on which to establish vegetation. Substandard practice at any time during the operational life of the site, its restoration and its aftercare can lead to tree planting schemes failing to achieve their desired effect. For example, inadequate compaction of waste can result in unacceptable levels of uneven settlement of the landfill. This can in turn lead to ponding of water, and escape of landfill gas or leachate into the rooting zone of trees, causing tree death (Chapter 2). Similarly, an inadequate depth of soil cover could predispose trees to drought stress and windthrow.

6.2 It is in the interests of the landfill operator to achieve high standards of restoration, both for the sake of pollution control and to provide an aesthetically pleasing landscape. Not only will this be environmentally sound, but it will also assist in winning the goodwill of the waste regulation and planning authorities, and local residents, thus helping to ensure the continued acceptability of this form of waste disposal.

Restoration phase

6.3 The restoration phase involves preparation of the site for an afteruse. It therefore includes the creation of the landform, installation of the landfill cap, and other pollution control measures (e.g. gas control), and placement of soil or soil-forming materials.

Cap type and thickness

6.4 A primary purpose of an engineered landfill cap is to reduce water percolation into waste, thereby minimising leachate generation (DoE, 1986). However, a cap will also facilitate the control and collection of landfill gas, and hinder its upward migration into the rooting zone of vegetation. Thus, a landfill cap is necessary both from a pollution control point of view and for protection of trees from landfill gas. The penetration of tree roots through a clay cap would therefore damage both the tree and the cap, and it is not in the interests of either the engineer or the forester for this to occur.

6.5 Clay is the most frequently used material for capping (Plate 2) though other natural materials such as bentonite and colliery shale, and synthetic materials such as HDPE are also used. Placement of a clay cap should not be undertaken in very wet weather, but sufficient moisture is necessary to ensure good compaction and accordingly spraying with water may sometimes be necessary. Maximum compaction can be achieved by placing the cap in layers no thicker than 0.3 m followed by rolling. A well compacted cap should have a bulk density in the region of 1.8–1.9 g cm^{-3}, a permeability of no greater than 1 x 10^{-7} cm s^{-1} (DoE, 1986) and a shrinkage potential of less than about 6.5% (see Chapter 5).

6.6 Waste Management Paper No. 26 (DoE, 1986) states that 'plant roots will rarely penetrate into light textured soils having a bulk density >1.7–1.8 g cm^{-3} or heavy textured soils with a bulk density >1.5–1.6'. There is nothing in the present review to contradict this viewpoint. It therefore seems likely that the high levels of compaction, and associated low oxygen levels in a clay cap will be sufficient to deter root growth (see Chapters 2 and 3). It seems unlikely that tree roots will be a primary cause of desiccation cracking in a clay cap covered by at least 1 m of soil, as they are unable to extract water from clays at the moisture tensions associated with cracking (see Chapter 5). It is possible that some tree roots could grow into existing fractures in a clay cap, but extension of roots into these cracks would seem unlikely if they provide a route for the escape of toxic landfill gases. Waste Management Paper No. 26 (DoE, 1986) recommends a clay thickness of 1 m and this review has not highlighted any reasons to alter this guidance.

6.7 Synthetic materials such as HDPE are increasingly seen as possible alternatives to clay for capping landfill sites. Although they have been relatively little used in this country to date, they are commonly used in the composite capping systems of countries such as Germany and Austria (Stief, 1989; Lechner, 1989). There is at present no information available on the growth of trees above a landfill capped with HDPE, but because of its high tensile strength it seems likely that HDPE will provide a total barrier to root penetration (see Chapter 3). Holes in synthetic materials produced during laying provide a means of escape for landfill gas rather than a means of entry into the waste for tree roots.

6.8 Provided the guidance outlined below on soil thickness and placement techniques is followed, the successful establishment of woodland above a clay or a synthetic cap should be possible without endangering cap integrity. It should be stressed again, however, that the success of the restoration phase will depend on good landfill design and operation. Poorly compacted waste can promote differential subsidence and cracking of the cap. This is undesirable with respect to leachate management, and can also be detrimental to tree growth if it results in ponding of water or escape of landfill gas into the rooting zone. Delaying tree planting for several years to allow remedial work to be carried out may overcome some of these problems (paragraph 6.25).

Gas control

6.9 Waste Management Paper No. 27 (DoE, 1991b) states that 'landfill gas should not be allowed to escape from a landfill in an unplanned or uncontrolled manner'. It therefore recommends that gas control measures should be installed on landfill sites containing biodegradable material, and describes the various types of system use for gas control, which include passive venting, active extraction, and utilisation (see Chapter 1). Landfill gas control systems are designed to ensure that migration of gas through cover materials is minimised. Thus they also help to prevent contamination of the rooting zone. It is especially important that gas control systems are installed where woodland is the planned afteruse as replacing dead trees is considerably more expensive than replacing other forms of vegetation such as grass.

6.10 Where woodland is a desired afteruse it will be important to ensure that woodland design incorporates allowance for routine sampling and access to boreholes, headgear and pipework. Gas wells are typically at 50 m spacing which allows blocks of woodland of approximately 0.25 ha to be planted. Rides between blocks may be necessary to allow access to below-ground pipes if wells are linked together.

Soil

Soil type

6.11 Soil is a scarce resource and obtaining sufficient quantities for final restoration of landfills is often difficult. However, one of the great advantages of woodland is that it can be established on materials which would not normally be considered as soil *sensu stricto* (DoE, 1986). This is because trees are less demanding in terms of nutrient requirements than agricultural crops. Thus, 'soil-forming materials' such as mineral over-burden, colliery shale, river dredgings, or soil separated from incoming wastes, can be acceptable alternatives to soil for establishing woodland, provided they meet certain minimum standards. The minimum standards proposed by Moffat and Bending (1992) are given in Table 6.1. Soil types not meeting these conditions may still be suitable for tree establishment, but species choice is likely to be severely restricted. Tree performance can be particularly disappointing when heavy clay is used as a soil-forming material.

6.12 Topsoil is not necessary for the establishment of woodland. Nevertheless, where topsoil is available it should be regarded as a very valuable resource which allows a much greater degree of flexibility in reclamation, especially in the choice of tree species (Moffat

Table 6.1 Minimum standards for soil-forming materials acceptable for woodland establishment on landfill sites (from Moffat and Bending, 1992).

Bulk density	<1.5 g cm^{-3} to at least 50 cm depth <1.7 g cm^{-3} to 1 m depth
Stoniness	<40% by volume. Few stones greater than 100 mm in size.
pH	4.0–8.0.
Electrical conductivity	<0.2 S m^{-1} (1:1 soil:water suspension)
Iron pyrite content	<0.05%
Heavy metal content	Not excessively over ICRCL (1987) threshold trigger concentrations
Organic contaminants	Not exceeding ICRCL (1987) action trigger concentrations

and McNeill, in press). If limited topsoil material is available for use on areas of a landfill site designated for woodland it should be spread as the uppermost soil layer, with a thickness of between 10–30 cm (see paragraph 3.34). Its placement should be related to the location of more demanding tree species in the planting scheme.

Soil placement

6.13 For successful tree establishment, soil cover on landfill sites must be loose and well aerated to facilitate root penetration and proliferation. Whilst trees can tolerate soils of low fertility, their growth is severely inhibited in soils with poor structure. **Compaction of soils is probably the most critical factor affecting tree growth and it should therefore be avoided wherever possible**. Compaction reduces the amount of water and gas movement into and through the soil (paragraph 3.28), and increases the forces holding water within the soils, thus reducing the availability of water to trees (paragraph 5.9). Furthermore, if the bulk density of soil is increased beyond certain limits roots cannot penetrate the soil (paragraphs 3.16–3.17).

6.14 Significant physical amelioration of compacted soil, especially at depths of more than 60 cm, can be extremely difficult to achieve. It is therefore best to implement soil placement techniques which avoid the creation of soil compaction. Soil materials are much more prone to compaction when worked wet, so all earth moving operations should be carried out during dry conditions when soils are friable. In addition, whilst earthscrapers are efficient at placing soils, they are generally inappropriate in areas designated for tree planting because they are particularly prone to causing soil compaction and smearing (Wilson, 1987). 'Loose-tipping' (Figure 6.1) is a technique which can almost entirely prevent soil compaction (DoE, 1986), and has been found to significantly improve survival, growth and stability of trees on reclaimed sites (Wilson, 1987; Bending, 1991). It is therefore strongly recommended that where a forestry or woodland afteruse is intended, soils should be loose-tipped.

6.15 The procedure for loose-tipping is described in detail in Waste Management Paper No. 26 (DoE, 1986). It involves the use of a tracked hydraulic excavator (backacter) and dump trucks, working from the surface of the cap (Figure 6.1). Soil is loaded from the stockpile into the dump trucks using hydraulic excavators or loaders. The dump trucks then transport the soil to the first strip to be restored, the width of which will be determined by the size and type of machinery available. The soil is tipped in heaps on the surface of the cap (Plate 12), and is spread and levelled by the excavator, also working from the cap surface. When the first strip has been laid, the second strip is started using the same cycle of operation. There is often no need to fully grade the restored surface as even ground is not necessary for woodland establishment. By this system of soil placement, trafficking of the restored soil profile is totally avoided, and compaction is reduced to a minimum.

1. Soil materials brought in by dump truck running over cap.

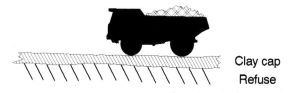

Clay cap
Refuse

2. Soil materials tipped in heaps onto cap.

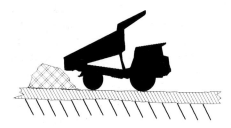

3. Soil materials spread and levelled by hydraulic excavator from cap surface.

Figure 6.1 Schematic diagram illustrating loose-tipping

6.16 Loose-tipped soils will encourage deeper rooting (Figure 3.5), thus improving wind stability, water and nutrient availability, and most importantly, shoot growth (Bending, 1991). Whilst some may perceive deeper rooting on loose-tipped soils over a landfill as creating a greater risk to cap integrity, the available evidence suggests that the looser the soil, the more marked will be the boundary between soil cover and the compact capping materials, and the less likely tree roots will be to cross it (Figure 3.6). **Roots only grow where conditions are favourable, so if cover soils are well structured, roots will have no incentive to grow into a compact, poorly aerated clay cap.**

Soil depth

6.17 The depth of soil required on landfill sites returned to a woodland afteruse will be determined by three factors:

50

- The need to prevent penetration of the landfill cap by tree roots.

- The need to prevent desiccation of the landfill cap by tree roots, if clay is the capping material used.

- The need to ensure sustained, healthy tree growth.

The available evidence suggests that tree roots are unable to exert a sufficient pressure to penetrate through a synthetic cap made of HDPE, or other similar materials with high tensile strength. Where landfill sites are capped with HDPE the depth of soil cover will therefore be governed solely by the requirements of the tree for water and anchorage. Thus for most parts of the country, 1 m of *rootable* soil cover will be adequate. A modelling exercise of the water requirements of mature tree crops (Moffat and McNeill, in press) suggests that this depth requirement may only need to be increased (to 1.5 m) in low rainfall areas of the south and east if the soil cover is particularly stony.

6.18 The high levels of compaction and low levels of oxygen found in a clay cap are likely to be sufficient to prevent root penetration (Chapter 3) and desiccation by roots (Chapter 5). Thus, as with HDPE, the depth of soil cover for woodland establishment over a clay, or other mineral, cap will be determined principally by the needs of the tree. However, because there are no direct observations of tree rooting habit on capped landfill sites a degree of caution must be exercised when recommending an appropriate soil depth. It seems likely that 1 m of soil cover would be perfectly sufficient to grow trees without danger to the cap. However, it is recommended that where landfill sites are protected by a clay cap, 1.5 m of *rootable* soil cover is provided in order to ensure an adequate level of insurance. This recommendation is considered a temporary one which may be modified in the light of future research. Clearly there is a financial implication to this recommendation which is considered in Chapter 7.

6.19 It is recognised that an additional 0.5 m of soil material may not always be easy to obtain. However, where woodland is to be established on part of a site, this extra depth will only be required on the particular area set aside for tree planting, and in many cases planting of a relatively small area of the landfill surface is sufficient to give a woodland effect. In addition, materials not normally considered soils can be acceptable as a growth medium for trees, provided they meet the minimum standards set out in Table 6.1.

6.20 Some concern has been expressed that if fine textured material (e.g heavy clay) is used as final soil cover, an increase in recommended depth from 1.0 m to 1.5 m could increase the depth of standing water above a cap. It is considered that an increased head of water above a mineral cap could promote higher rates of percolation. A well compacted cap complying with the specifications set out in Waste Management Paper No. 26 (DoE, 1986) should have a permeability of 1×10^{-7} cm s^{-1} or less (i.e. a percolation rate of about 30 mm per year). If an increased head of water were to double the percolation rate, which is unlikely, the amount of water entering the site would still be only about 60 mm per year. According to Knox (1991) it is not desirable to maintain a head of water above a clay cap at all as this would increase percolation significantly. Rather, measures should be taken to ensure drainage of excess water from above the cap.

Landform and drainage

6.21 It is important that the landform of a restored landfill site is designed sympathetically in order to blend in with the local landscape. If this is not possible, then a more emphatic approach may be necessary (Forestry Commission, 1991) whereby a distinct, but visually pleasing, landform is created. It is also important that the landform is designed to encourage the shedding of surface water, so that soil waterlogging and ingress of water into the landfill is minimised. In general, post-settlement gradients in the region of 1 in 30 (2°) have been found to be adequate for most afteruses (DoE, 1986), though slopes of 1 in 10 (5.5–6.0°) have been recommended for forestry on reclaimed mineral sites (Wilson, 1985). Whilst slopes of 1 in 3 (18°) are the maximum for uphill use of most forest machinery, gradients as steep as this are not recommended, especially where synthetic materials are used for capping, as this could lead to an increased likelihood of soil slippage. On long slopes with gradients greater than 1 in 10 soil erosion may be prevented by the use of cut-off berms every 20–30 m, but the necessity for such measures will depend on substrate type. After soils are

placed a low maintenance grass sward should be established as soon as possible to minimise erosion risk and rainfall percolation.

6.22 Sufficient gradients and the placement of soils by loose-tipping (paragraph 6.13) will encourage good drainage by allowing rapid lateral movement of water. Knox (1991) has suggested drainage could be further improved by the incorporation of a drainage layer above the cap. He suggested that this measure could reduce percolation to as low as 20 mm per year, even if the hydraulic conductivity of the cap is as high as 1×10^{-6} cm s^{-1}. A DoE-funded review of landfill cover systems in the UK, Europe and the USA indicates that a drainage layer is increasingly becoming a requirement of modern landfill design in Europe (MRM Partnership, personal communication). For example, in the Netherlands, guidance issued by the Ministry of Housing, Physical Planning and the Environment (NMHPPE, 1991) specifies that a drainage layer of permeable sand no less than 0.3 m thick, and containing a drainage system, should be placed above the landfill cap. A specified purpose of this layer is to protect the cap against damage due to root growth (see paragraph 3.26) and burrowing animals. In addition, a coarse layer above the cap could serve to prevent water movement out of the cap through the creation of a barrier to capillary rise (Ward, 1975). If the drainage layer is protected from fines by geotextiles such as Terram 2000, this will also serve to prevent roots from entering the drainage layer (Brennan et al., 1989) and thus will also protect the cap from root penetration. The trees themselves could be beneficial to landfill hydrology because of their potential to reduce water input into soil cover compared with grass or agricultural crops (Chapter 5).

Completion of restoration

6.23 A major problem on landfill sites is the occurrence of subsidence. Where subsidence leads to ponding, remedial filling is often necessary. It is important that the five year aftercare period for the planned afteruse (paragraph 1.8) does not begin until all the activities necessary to complete the restoration have been undertaken. If tree planting is the intended final afteruse, and remedial works are predicted for some years, then temporary restoration to some other form of vegetation is recommended. It may be appropriate to delay the placement of the final soil cover until the majority of settlement and any necessary maintenance has taken place. In the case of new proposals for landfill sites, it is recommended that conditions specifying an extended management period to cover interim restoration, prior to the formal 5 year aftercare period, should be considered as part of the planning permission. In the cases where there is existing planning permission a voluntary management agreement (Section 106, Town and Country Planning Act 1990) may need to be sought to ensure that the usual requirement for a 5 year aftercare period following tree planting is honoured.

Aftercare phase

6.24 The aftercare period is designed to ensure that the restored land achieves the required standard for the planned afteruse. For land-uses including a woodland component it involves operations such as cultivation, planting, weed control, protection from animals, fertilising, and irrigation.

Timing of tree planting

6.25 It may be desirable from a landscape point of view, or it may be a condition of the planning permission (or for some older mineral workings with modern waste management licences, a condition of the site licence) that trees are planted as soon as possible after soil has been placed. However, in some cases it may be prudent to delay tree planting for some years. As discussed above (paragraph 6.23), differential settlement leading to ponding of surface water may necessitate remedial infilling. In addition, maintenance of gas and leachate control systems may necessitate excavation of pipework below the soil surface. There is little point in planting trees in situations where they could be buried by further infilling or may need to be removed to enable access to pipework and headgear. On sites which are relatively shallow, where filling is predominantly with inert material, or where subsidence is minimised by suitable cell design and effective waste compaction, early tree planting may be possible. However, on deeper sites with a higher proportion of biodegradable material, longer periods between capping and planting may be necessary. It is impractical to recommend an all-embracing timeframe for tree planting

on landfill sites as each site is unique. However, as settlement tends to be greatest in the first 2–4 years, and may continue for 10 years or longer depending on the depth of waste and its rate of decomposition, it is likely that a delay of 2 years or more may be necessary on some sites.

Cultivation

6.26 If the recommendations for soil placement are followed (paragraph 6.15), cultivation should not be needed. However, if loose-tipping of soil materials has not been carried out, or if consolidation has taken place after soil placement, cultivation must be carried out to relieve compaction. Cultivation of compacted soils may be necessary initially to establish a grass sward if temporary restoration is carried out (paragraph 6.23), and in this event it is likely that further cultivation may also be required in the season before tree planting (pre-planting ripping).

6.27 The most effective form of cultivation for tree establishment is the ripping of soils to depths of about 0.5–0.75 m. Agricultural machinery is rarely powerful enough to enable ripping to this depth, so a tracked dozer (300+ hp) should be used with three tines mounted in a parallelogram linkage; the outer-most tines positioned behind the dozer tracks to counteract any compaction caused by the dozer. 'Winged' tines are more effective in relieving compaction than conventional tines (Binns and Fourt, 1981). Ripping should only be carried out downslope during dry weather when the subsoil is relatively dry (May to September). Ripping a wet soil simply forms a subsurface channel and fails to cause the desired heaving and shattering necessary to improve soil structure (Moffat, 1989).

Species selection

6.28 The first rule of species selection is to choose a species that will actually grow on a particular site. So, for example, there is little point in selecting demanding species such as beech or hornbeam which tend to be intolerant of the conditions on man-made sites. Similarly, birch is inappropriate for planting on sites with a high soil pH, and ash is inappropriate for soils with a low pH. Other factors which may be more or less important in deciding which trees to plant include the ability of trees to withstand windthrow, to fit into the wider landscape, to be a native species (Appendix 2), or to provide a timber crop. On phased landfill sites, selection can be modified through experience gained of tree performance on earlier restored phases.

Matching species to site

6.29 The aim of species selection is to match tree species to site conditions. Failure to do this can result in checked growth and/or heavy losses and the need for expensive replanting. Thus, selection of trees for landfill sites should only be made after a thorough evaluation of actual or expected site conditions. A knowledge of the ability of different trees to tolerate heavy clay (probably seasonally waterlogged),

calcareous, or acidic soils will be helpful for deciding on appropriate species. A knowledge of tolerance to exposure may also be useful where sites have little shelter or are influenced by salt-laden coastal winds. In addition, tolerance of air pollution may be a desirable feature of trees for planting on sites near to heavy industry (see paragraph 2.28).

6.30 Table 6.2 lists the tree species most likely to grow well on restored landfill sites, and gives an indication of their relative ability to tolerate adverse soil conditions, exposure, and air pollution. A survey of 19 landfill sites in England during the summer of 1991 (Appendix 1) suggested that alder, birch, wild cherry, English oak, field maple, Norway maple, sycamore, Turkey oak and willow may be

Table 6.2 Trees most likely to tolerate conditions on landfill sites. Species are classified as tolerant (••), moderately tolerant (•), or intolerant (x) to heavy soils (likely to be seasonally waterlogged), calcareous soils, acidic soils, exposure, and air pollution. Scientific names of tree species may be found in Appendix 2.

Species	Heavy soils	Calcareous soils	Acidic soils	Exposure	Air pollution	Comments
Broadleaves						
Ash	x	••	x	x	x	More fertile sites only
Common alder	••	•	•	•	••	Nitrogen-fixing
Crack willow	••	••	x	x	•	
Downy birch	•	•	•	••	••	Tolerates low fertility
English oak	•	•	•	•	•	More fertile sites only
False acacia	•	•	••	x	••	Nitrogen-fixing. South only
Field maple	•	••	•	•	•	
Goat willow	•	•	•	x	••	
Grey alder	••	•	•	•	•	Nitrogen-fixing
Grey poplar	••	••	•	••	••	
Hawthorn	•	•	•	••	•	Tolerates browsing
Italian alder	•	••	x	x	••	Nitrogen-fixing
Norway maple	•	••	x	••	•	
Red alder	••	x	•	••	•	Nitrogen-fixing
Red oak	•	•	••	•	•	
Rowan	•	•	•	••	•	
Silver birch	x	x	••	••	••	Tolerates low fertility
Swedish whitebeam	••	•	•	•	•	
Sycamore	•	••	•	••	••	
Turkey oak	••	•	•	•	•	
Whitebeam	•	••	••	•	•	
White poplar	••	x	•	•	••	
Wild cherry	x	•	x	x	•	More fertile sites only
Conifers						
Corsican pine	•	••	••	••	••	Below 250 m O.D.
European larch	•	x	•	•	x	
Japanese larch	•	x	•	•	•	
Leyland cypress	•	•	•	••	••	Mainly for shelter
Lodgepole pine	•	x	••	•	x	North only
Scots pine	x	x	••	••	x	

especially worthy of consideration. Beech and hornbeam were notable for their poor performance. A general rule for planting on reclaimed sites is that 'pioneer' species should be used in preference to 'climax' species.

Windthrow hazard

6.31 Windthrow hazard is least in the lowlands of the south and east and greatest in the uplands of the north and west (Figures 4.1 and 4.2). Exposed upland sites are the most likely to experience winds of exceptional force and will tend to have a high score for windthrow hazard (see Chapter 4). In such areas it may be advisable to select tree species which are relatively small (usually <15 m) at maturity (Table 4.8) and tolerate exposure (Table 6.2), or to avoid tree planting altogether. Where trees are planted, increasing the depth of soil cover to 2 m should ensure that even if windthrow does occur, the cap would not be exposed. Additionally, if soils are loose-tipped, as recommended in paragraph 6.14, windthrow hazard will be greatly reduced over conventional soil placement techniques (Bending, 1991).

6.32 Managing woodland as coppice will reduce the risk of windthrow to negligible levels, and could be an especially useful system of woodland management in areas of high windthrow hazard. Most broadleaves can be coppiced (Evans, 1984), but oak is the only traditionally coppiced species suggested as being suitable for planting on landfill sites. Short rotation coppice normally involves the planting of rapidly growing willow and poplar clones, and there is limited evidence to suggest that poplar trees which have been coppiced may have smaller root systems than standard trees (paragraph 3.39).

Rooting depth

6.33 There is little evidence from the literature to indicate any genetically-determined differences in rooting depth between tree species (though there may be differences in root system architecture) on well aerated soils of good structure (Chapter 3). However, species do vary in their ability to tolerate unfavourable soil conditions. This means that species less tolerant of adverse soil conditions tend to produce shallow root systems with a greater frequency than more tolerant species. Thus, for example, birch, Norway spruce and sycamore

have usually been found to have a relatively shallow root system whilst that of common alder is more often deeper (Table 3.1). Nevertheless, the compacted nature of a clay cap suggests that there need be no restrictions on species selection, provided the guidelines for cap design, soil placement and soil thickness are followed.

Stock type

6.34 The success of any scheme for establishing woodland on a landfill site will depend ultimately on the type and quality of the planting stock used. Block plantings designed to give a woodland effect should generally be carried out using nursery transplants. The recommended plant type for the bulk of woodland and forestry planting is the bare-root transplant. These plants establish quickly and begin to make rapid growth often in the first year of planting. Generally the preference is for shorter but sturdier plants on exposed sites while slightly larger ones can be used on more fertile sites with less exposure. Establishment of sensitive species such as Corsican pine can be greatly improved using containerised stock (Crowther *et al.*, 1991).

6.35 Observations over a range of landfill sites (Appendix 1) confirm the unsuitability of large tree stock such as whips or standards for woodland establishment due to their much poorer performance compared with transplants. They are more expensive than transplants, are difficult to establish, and often make very poor growth during the first few years after planting.

Plant handling and planting procedure

6.36 Careful plant handling and correct planting procedure are critical if trees are to survive the initial shock of transplanting and produce rapid growth. Bad handling can result in significant deaths even before the trees reach the planting site (Insley, 1980). Of particular importance is the need to keep the roots moist at all times, as exposure of the root system to drying can kill even the larger roots in a few hours. It is therefore normal practice to keep plants in polythene bags in a cool, shaded place during transfer from the nursery to the planting site. To avoid desiccation, the trees must be kept in a planting bag until the moment of planting.

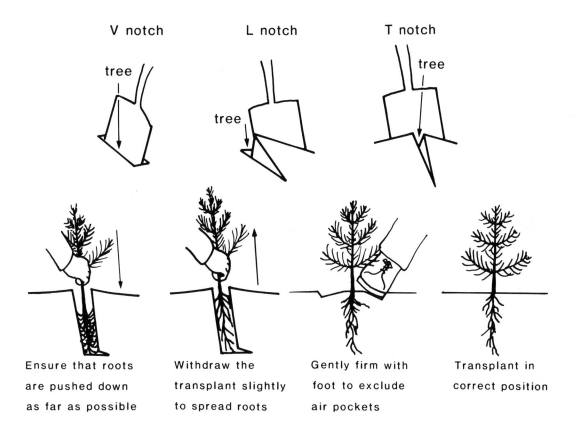

V notch　　**L notch**　　**T notch**

Ensure that roots
are pushed down
as far as possible

Withdraw the
transplant slightly
to spread roots

Gently firm with
foot to exclude
air pockets

Transplant in
correct position

Figure 6.2 Diagram to illustrate procedure for notch planting of trees.

6.37 Bare-rooted transplants are usually notch-planted (Figure 6.2). Slits are cut in the soil and held open with a spade while the tree's roots are carefully inserted so that they spread downwards. The soil is then firmed with the foot to provide secure anchorage. On very clayey sites, notably those where landfilling has followed from brick clay extraction, pit-planting may be necessary because slits re-open in dry weather and roots become exposed. Smearing of the pit face should be avoided.

6.38 A number of factors, including site characteristics and choice of species, influence tree spacing, but a distance of 2 m is normal in British forestry. This gives a stocking density of 2500 plants per hectare. On landfill sites, where tree survival and growth may be relatively poorer, closer spacing may be advisable.

6.39 Timing of planting is also important. The planting season for trees is usually considered to be late November to early March. It has been shown that trees planted early in the dormant season (November) can develop twice as much root by full leafing out compared with those planted towards the end of the planting season (March) (Gilbertson *et al.,* 1987). This means that early-planted trees are likely to be more able to tolerate spring drought than late-planted trees. However, on other sites, planting later in the season may be more appropriate e.g. in clay soils which may be waterlogged for much of the winter. Planting into frozen ground should be avoided.

Weed control

6.40 Grasses and leguminous herbs are usually sown on newly restored landfill sites to reduce soil erosion and to improve site appearance. Although deliberately established, these plants are 'weeds' as far as the newly planted tree is concerned, because they are strong competitors for moisture and nutrients (Davies, 1987).

55

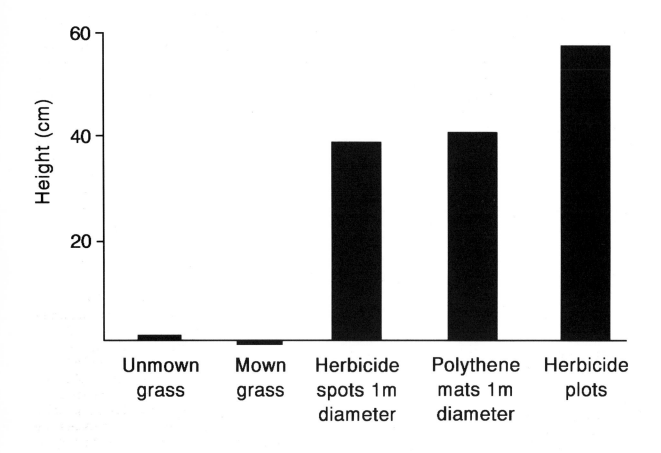

Figure 6.3 Effect of weed control on the first year height growth of silver maple.

Young trees planted into a grass sward often show classic stress symptoms: sparse small leaves, shoot dieback, and a yellowing or browning of leaves caused by nitrogen deficiency and water stress respectively (Potter, 1989). Experiments have unequivocally shown that tree survival and growth is significantly reduced by the presence of weeds (Figure 6.3; Plates 13 and 14), and it is clear that mowing or cutting is an ineffective means of controlling them. Indeed, it has been demonstrated that mowing increases the vigour of a grass sward, thereby increasing soil moisture deficits and decreasing tree vigour (Davies, 1987).

6.41 There are several methods of controlling weeds around newly planted trees, but to be effective it is essential that weeds are killed or removed entirely. The careful use of herbicide is an effective and economical method of weed control. Mulching has also been found to be effective by smothering or preventing the establishment of weeds. Mulch mats made of

black polythene (Plate 15) have been found to be most effective as they are able to prevent light reaching the soil and remain impenetrable for 2–3 years (Potter, 1989). Experiments have shown that a minimum weed-free area required around a newly planted tree is a 1 m diameter spot. Ideally, weed control should start before the trees are planted, and the area immediately around the base of the tree should be kept weed free for 3–4 years.

6.42 A combination of glyphosate (all year application) and propyzamide (winter application) are generally recommended for weed control in the forest (Williamson and Lane, 1989). However, on landfill sites without the provision of topsoil, care must be taken in the choice of herbicide, especially those which are soil-acting. Propyzamide is less effective on soils which are rich in organic matter, so smaller application rates than those used in conventional forestry may be necessary where soil-forming materials contain little or no organic matter.

Protection from animals

6.43 Damage to trees by bark stripping, browsing or burrowing can be caused by a number of small and large mammals, including voles, rabbits, squirrels, and deer. Trees can be killed or seriously damaged if they are not adequately protected from these animals. For small-scale planting, individual tree protection with vole guards, rabbit guards or plastic mesh may be appropriate, depending on the animal populations likely to frequent the site (Potter, 1989). Good weed control around trees can also discourage the activity of voles which dislike crossing areas of open ground. Treeshelters offer a high degree of protection from mammal damage, and have the added advantage of providing a favourable microclimate around the tree by acting as a mini-greenhouse (Potter, 1991). Where blocks of woodland greater than 2 ha are planned, the most cost-effective protection is exclusion by means of fencing (Pepper, 1992). Spring steel wire is now recommended for all forest fences as it has the advantage that once tensioned it can accept further 'accidental' tensioning from animals or humans without deforming. Once the accidental load is removed the fence returns to its original position and tension (Pepper, 1992). This property may also be useful on landfill sites where differential settlement may alter fencing tension. Nevertheless, fences should be regularly checked to ensure their continuing effectiveness.

Beating up

6.44 Some losses after planting are almost inevitable, and may be due to such things as poor stock quality, bad planting practice, mammal, insect or fungal attack, drought, waterlogging or landfill gas. If losses of greater than 10% are incurred, beating up (the process of replacing trees that have died soon after planting) should be undertaken. If tree losses occur in large groups, it may be important to evaluate the reasons for failure prior to beating up. Beating up should be carried out as soon as possible as any delay will extend the period over which weed control will be needed, and will increase the risk of the new trees being suppressed by the original planting stock. The adoption of high standards of tree handling and planting should ensure that the need for beating up is minimised or even eliminated.

Irrigation

6.45 In areas of the country which receive little summer rainfall, or where soils have poor moisture availability, irrigation of young trees may be required to prevent the large scale failures that have been experienced on some sites in the past. In addition, on shrinkable clays which can experience extensive surface cracking, tree roots can be exposed. Good weed control reduces and often eliminates the need for irrigation (Potter, 1989). If irrigation is required, it is important that water of acceptable quality is used. Water with a high soluble salt content can sometimes do more harm than good (see paragraph 5.30).

Fertiliser application

6.46 Soil materials used as final cover on restored landfill sites often suffer from a lack of available nitrogen and phosphorus which are essential for healthy tree growth (Moffat and McNeill, in press). It is therefore advisable to choose species tolerant of infertility for planting on such sites (Table 6.2). If species intolerant of low fertility are planted, or the site is especially poor in nutrients, deficiency symptoms may be expressed. For example, nitrogen deficiency in conifers results in a general reduction of growth, yellowing of foliage, and the production of a thin and spindly leading shoot. Phosphorus deficiency leads to poor height growth coupled with decreased needle length and a dullish green colour. In broadleaves, the effect of nitrogen deficiency is to reduce leaf size and cause a general yellowing of the crown, and phosphorus deficiency results in the production of dull stunted leaves (Binns *et al.*, 1980). Nutrient deficiencies can be diagnosed accurately by means of foliar analysis, and this technique can also be used to devise appropriate fertiliser application strategies.

6.47 For some substrates used as soil-forming materials it is possible to predict with some confidence the probable nutrient deficiencies that trees may experience. For example, colliery shale can often be deficient in the macro-nutrients nitrogen and phosphorus. Whilst fertiliser application is not normally recommended within the first 2–3 years after planting in conventional forestry, recent evidence suggests that moderate applications of fertiliser can have some benefits to tree growth even in the first year of growth on difficult sites (Gilbertson *et al.*, 1987). Early applications of fertiliser on sites known to be nutrient deficient may therefore be beneficial. Inorganic fertilisers may not be needed to rectify nutrient deficiencies, as cheaper alternatives which could be quite acceptable on landfill sites are available. The most obvious alternative is sewage sludge which is freely available and contains useful amounts of both N and P. Its high organic content can also improve soil structure (Moffat, 1988). The practicalities of sludge application in woodland are dealt with in detail by Wolstenholme *et al.* (1992).

Management phase

The need for woodland management

6.48 Although in many cases woodland, once established, can be left to grow, continuing management is often essential. The type of management will depend to a large extent on the objectives of the woodland. Thus, plantings designed to give a commercial timber crop may require cleaning (the removal of unwanted woody vegetation), pruning (the removal of branches to improve timber quality), and thinning (the removal of a proportion of trees in order to increase the diameter increment of the remainder). Woodland managed for nature conservation may require the removal of certain invasive weed species, or the encouragement of more desirable, but less vigorous species. Edges are especially valuable for enriching and retaining wildlife, and with sensitive management a rich flora and fauna can often be sustained. Coppice has high wildlife value but needs to be cut every few years, depending on rotation length. Woodland managed for amenity and public access may require operations such as the laying and maintenance of footpaths, cutting of grass, and litter control. In all cases where they are used, fences, individual tree guards and treeshelters will need to be maintained in an effective condition during their design life.

6.49 Poor aftercare and management of a landfill site will result in a neglected, untidy and unsightly appearance no matter how good or bad the quality of operations in the restoration phase.

Monitoring

6.50 Sites should be monitored to assess tree survival, and beat up requirements, and for larger, phased, landfill sites to enable improved species selection for later phases. Because there is little direct experience of tree growth on modern landfill sites, it is also recommended that, until further data become available, an investigation of tree rooting depth from time to time should be incorporated into a monitoring regime to check whether any roots are penetrating the engineered cap. It is suggested that a 5 year interval between inspections may be appropriate and that monitoring continues for up to 20 years, by which time tree root systems should be fully developed. A method that has been found to be highly effective for examining vertical root distribution on landfill sites is the excavation of a trench about 1 m from the base of the tree with a small hydraulic excavator. Examination of the trench wall indicates the presence or absence, depth and thickness of roots. If roots can be seen penetrating into the cap it may be necessary to carefully remove some or all of the trees. In the design of tree layout it may therefore be important to allow access to enable root excavations to be performed. This recommendation is considered a temporary one, which should be rendered unnecessary as experience of the behaviour of trees on modern landfill sites increases.

Summary and conclusions

6.51 This report suggests that woodland can be successfully established on landfill sites provided that high standards of landfill practice and a high quality of restoration are achieved. The need to ensure the highest standards of silvicultural practice and aftercare management must also not be neglected. The main conclusions and recommendations outlined in this chapter to achieve a successful restoration to a woodland afteruse are outlined in the following paragraphs:

6.52 A low permeability cap should be installed over the deposited waste, in conjunction with a gas control system, as these measures will prevent contamination of the tree root zone with landfill gas.

6.53 In order to prevent penetration of a clay cap by tree roots the cap should be compacted to achieve a bulk density of 1.8 g cm^{-3} or greater (this level of compaction is necessary in order to obtain a permeability of 1×10^{-7} cm s^{-1}). Tree roots will not penetrate through an intact cap made from synthetic materials of high tensile strength such as HDPE.

6.54 Sufficient final gradients are required to facilitate the rapid shedding of surface water. Gradients of 1 in 30 are considered a minimum for the establishment of woodland and steeper gradients may be necessary if heavy soil materials, prone to waterlogging, are used in the restoration. A coarse drainage layer placed above the cap will speed up the removal of excess water and can help to reduce percolation into the landfill. In addition, a drainage layer will provide a greater degree of protection of a clay cap from tree roots.

6.55 Topsoil is not necessary for woodland establishment, although its use will allow a greater degree of flexibility in species choice and is likely to significantly improve tree growth. Materials not normally considered soils (e.g. overburden, mineral spoil) can be adequate as final cover for tree planting provided they meet minimum standards (see Table 6.1).

6.56 Soil placement should be by loose-tipping to avoid compaction. If compaction is unavoidable or if soil reconsolidates after loose-tipping, cultivation by deep ripping must be carried out prior to tree planting.

6.57 A minimum depth of soil cover of 1 m is recommended where landfill sites are capped with HDPE or similar synthetic materials. This depth will provide adequate anchorage and moisture reserves for trees in most parts of the country. In areas of the country with a high windthrow hazard, or in the extreme south and east of the country if cover soils are particularly stony, this depth may need to be increased to 1.5 m. Where sites are capped with compacted clays or other mineral materials, a soil depth of 1.5 m is recommended to ensure protection of the cap. This recommendation is considered temporary and is a maximum for added safety. It may be revised in the light of future research.

6.58 Once the cap has been placed and covered, it may be prudent to delay placement of final soil cover and tree planting for 2 or more years to allow for servicing of pipework, headgear, access to sampling boreholes, and any remedial filling that may be required to counteract the effects of settlement. Under these circumstances the formal aftercare period should not begin until the site is ready for planting.

6.59 Species selection must match species to site. Failure to do so can result in poor survival and growth. Factors such as susceptibility to windthrow, tolerance of exposure and difficult soil conditions may need to be taken into account. On phased sites, an evaluation of the success of establishment on earlier restored phases will enable improved selection for later phases. There is little evidence to suggest that any tree species is intrinsically deep or shallow rooting. Rooting depth will depend upon soil conditions, and will be restricted to the depth of soil above the cap.

6.60 Transplants or small containerised stock are recommended for the establishment of woodland. Large whips and standards are generally unsuitable.

6.61 Careful plant handling, correct planting procedure, and efficient weed control are essential to successful woodland establishment on landfill sites. Protection from animals, irrigation and fertilisation may also be important components of post-planting maintenance.

6.62 Once established, woodland should be managed so that it achieves its full potential, whether for timber production, landscape enhancement, recreation, wildlife value, or all of these. Poor aftercare management will result in an unsightly and untidy site no matter how good or bad the quality of operations in the restoration phase.

Chapter 7

Economics

Introduction

7.1 The establishment of woodland on landfill sites may have quite different financial implications from restoration to other land uses such as grassland. An evaluation of financial costs, and benefits of establishing and maintaining woodland should therefore be incorporated into the decision-making framework associated with the planning of a landfill site afteruse. As part of the decision-making process it may also be important to take into account the social implications of any proposed afteruse.

Costs of woodland establishment

Financial implications of recommendations for soil depth

7.2 Waste Management Paper No. 26 (DoE, 1986) suggests that 1 m of soil is usually adequate to protect a clay landfill cap. However, in Chapter 6 it was recommended that 1.5 m of soil or soil-forming materials would be necessary for the establishment of woodland on landfill sites capped with clay. This would therefore require the provision of an additional 0.5 m of soil materials. If the provision of this extra cover were to be made at the expense of void space, this could result in a potential loss of revenue of about £50 000 per ha (assuming 1 m³ void space is worth £10) plus the costs of providing the extra soil materials. However, it should be remembered that trees can grow on poor quality substrates (paragraph 6.11), *including* those for which a disposal charge could be levied. Thus, if revenue could be generated from waste that could be used as cover material (e.g. quarry waste, colliery spoil, PFA), the provision of the necessary depth of soil for woodland establishment may not incur any net increase in costs. Capping a site with HDPE will avoid the necessity of providing 1.5 m of cover materials (paragraph 6.17).

Planting and maintenance costs

7.3 Estimates of likely costs for woodland establishment on a landfill site are illustrated in Table 7.1. It must be recognised, however, that these costs can vary considerably depending on a number of factors. Fencing, or the provision of treeshelters, is likely to be one of the major costs. The price of fencing is usually in the region of £4–6 m⁻¹, but where woods are smaller than 2 ha, the use of treeshelters can be more economical (Crowther *et al.*, 1991). Treeshelters can also help to reduce the costs of weed control by allowing more rapid herbicide application because less care needs to be taken to protect the tree stem from herbicide contact. If the site is already fenced, further fencing may not be necessary and this could almost halve establishment costs. Another factor affecting costs is the soil type: the speed of planting is usually slower, and hence planting costs are higher, on compact or stony soil. The purchase price of broadleaves is usually greater than that of conifers.

Table 7.1 Estimated total costs at 1992 prices (per ha) for establishing and maintaining broadleaved woodland on a landfill site, assuming a 5 year establishment period. (Purchase price of conifers is slightly lower).

	£ per ha
Establishment	
Fencing (labour and materials)	1200
Planting (3,000 trees per ha)	
Trees	600
Labour	360
Preplanting weed control (labour and materials)	120
Maintenance	
Beating up	
Trees	150
Labour	150
Weed control (4 year period)	720
TOTAL	3300

Benefits of woodland establishment

7.4 The costs of establishing woodland may be offset against potential sources of income such as the Forestry Commission's (Forestry Authority) Woodland Grant Scheme and, in the longer term, revenue from sales of woodland products (Plate 16). There are also systems for putting a monetary value on the benefits of woodland such as landscape, wildlife, amenity or recreation.

Woodland Grant Scheme

7.5 The Forestry Commission's Woodland Grant Scheme (WGS) was introduced in 1988 to encourage the creation of new forests and woodlands through the provision of financial assistance with planting and maintenance. All woodland, including coppice and short rotation coppice, is eligible for consideration for grants under the scheme. Normal threshold qualifications for the WGS are that areas designated for woodland should not be less than 0.25 ha in size or less than 15 m in width. There are two groups of grants available. The first is the *establishment grant* which is designed to assist planting, and the second is the *management grant* which helps with the subsequent maintenance of woodland.

7.6 Application forms can be obtained from, and should be returned to, the local Forestry Authority office. The application should describe the type of woodland proposed, the long-term objectives of the woodland, and work proposed during the initial 5 year establishment period to meet these objectives. A map of the proposed planting area is required, which for small areas should be on a scale of 1:2500. After examination of the proposal and a visit to the site, the proposal will either be accepted, modified or rejected. Once the proposals are acceptable, a contract is signed under which the owner undertakes to manage the woodland to an agreed standard throughout the grant period.

7.7 The rates of grants for woodland establishment as at August 1992 are given in Table 7.2. Higher rates of grant are paid for broadleaved species and native Scots pine within its former natural distribution in Scotland. Smaller areas of woodland are eligible for higher grants in recognition of the higher costs normally incurred, for example for fencing.

Payment is in three instalments, 70% on completion of the planting, with further instalments of 20% and 10% at 5-yearly intervals thereafter, subject to satisfactory establishment and maintenance.

Table 7.2 Rates of establishment grants under the Woodland Grant Scheme as at August 1992.

	£ per ha	
Grant band	Conifers	Broadleaves
Less than 1.0 ha	1005	1575
1.0–2.9 ha	880	1375
3.0–9.9 ha	795	1175
10 ha and over	615	975

7.8 Landfill sites which were restored to an agricultural afteruse (arable or grassland) prior to 1987 may be eligible for a Better Land Supplement (£400 per ha for conifers and £600 per ha for broadleaves) if a change of landuse to forestry is proposed.

7.9 A Community Woodland Supplement of £950 per ha is also available under the Woodland Grant Scheme, subject to certain conditions being met. To be eligible, proposals must be within 5 miles of the edge of a town or city, and in an area where the opportunities for woodland recreation are limited. In addition, it is a condition of the supplement that there should be free public access. Woodland established with the support of the supplement will also be eligible for a special management grant from age 11 onwards.

7.10 Standard management grants are available to assist with woodland maintenance once trees are 11 years old. An annual payment is made in return for a 5 year management plan, agreed with and monitored by the Forestry Authority. Such plans are expected to increase the environmental value of the woodland, as well as dealing with normal maintenance operations. Standard rates of grant are £10 per ha for conifers and £15 per ha for broadleaves, paid annually during the period of the 5 year management agreement. An annual supplement of £5 and £10 per ha is paid for conifers and broadleaves respectively where the size of the woodland is less than 10 ha. In addition, a further payment of £10 per ha per year is available for woods that qualify for the Community Woodland Supplement.

Income from woodland products

7.11 The UK provides only 13% of its own requirements for woodland products. Demand has grown faster than supply for a number of years so that volumes of imported wood are still increasing (Cunningham, 1991). There is therefore a large potential market for home-produced woodland products. All logs over 14 cm top diameter can be regarded as potential sawlog material (Greig and Thompson, 1991), which can be sold to sawmills for conversion into sawn timber. The highest prices are paid for hardwood sawlogs, usually for the production of veneer. Logs not good enough for veneer may make joinery grade timber, while logs of poorer grade are normally converted to fencing material or mining timber. Sawlogs are not the only forest products that can be sold to generate income. Everything from small roundwood to branches and bark has a potential market (Table 7.3), although the sizes and availability of these markets vary considerably. As a guide to possible revenue from timber sales on reclaimed sites, Moffat and McNeill (in press) have suggested that an alder crop might be thinned after about 15–20 years, and clearfelled after 40 years to yield between 150–200 cubic metres of wood per ha, and a financial return of £1500–2000 per ha (1992 prices). Nevertheless, actual timber value will depend to a large extent on proximity to local, regional and national markets, current price levels, and demand. Forestry consultants can prepare production estimates, measure and value timber and provide marketing and general management advice.

7.12 Even if woods are managed for other purposes than a commercial timber crop, e.g. nature conservation, recreation, amenity, they can still generate an income from thinnings which are likely to be necessary from time to time. Whilst many markets for woodland products are already established, such as the production of fences and pallets, there are many more which remain to be established and exploited. For example, although short rotation coppice has the potential to produce up to 15 tonnes per ha per year and could yield a financial return similar to that of an arable crop, the market for fuel wood in the UK at present is strictly limited. Nevertheless, if a regular supply were to become available at a competitive price with fossil fuels, the market should grow rapidly. On larger landfill sites it may be economic to install equipment to generate energy from biomass to supplement energy produced from landfill gas.

Table 7.3 Potential markets for woodland products.

Poles	Barn poles
	Rustic poles
	Pit props
Pulpwood	Paper products
Fencing	Post and rail for stock control
	Forest fences to exclude stock, rabbits and deer
	Roadside and motorway fences
	Domestic garden and urban fences – mostly panelled
	Pallet wood
	Industrial pallets
Wood based panel products	Particle board
	Medium density fibre board
	Oriented strand board
	Hardboard
Woodchips and bark	Mulch
	Compost
	Paths and playgrounds
	Race-courses and stables
	Fuel
Rural crafts	Carving
	Furniture
	Hurdles and fences
	Ladders
	Turnery
	Garden products
Fuel	Firewood
	Charcoal
	Boilers (chipped wood)
Short rotation coppice	Fuel
	Particle board
	Pulpwood
Other	Christmas trees

7.13 Finding and exploiting markets may require some imagination and marketing ability, but with some effort it should be possible to generate a useful income. Information on markets for woodland products on a county basis can be obtained from the Forestry Commission in the publication *Marketing for Small Woodlands* (Forestry Commission, 1990).

Non-wood benefits of woodland

7.14 Forests and woodlands can be a valuable source of marketable woodland products. However, to obtain a true reflection of the actual worth of an area of woodland, the additional benefits such as recreation, amenity, wildlife conservation, and their ability to act as a 'carbon sink' should also be taken into account.

Keeble (1991) has stressed the importance of allowing early public access to restored landfill sites, so that by enjoying the benefits that a well restored site can provide, the public status of the industry can be enhanced.

7.15 The value of woodland products is reflected by a market price but the social value of woodland is not. It has been argued that if both items are of value then why should one benefit have a market price and not the other? This argument has been acknowledged by the National Audit Office who suggest that the social benefits should be taken into account as well as the financial ones in an economic assessment of forestry (NAO, 1986). Bateman (1991) has proposed the assessment of all the benefits of woodland, both priced and unpriced, to obtain its total social value. By applying cost-benefit analysis to woodland, involving both a *financial appraisal* and a *social appraisal*, it is possible to come up with a figure for *total economic value* (TEV). There have been various attempts to attach monetary values to the social appraisal, and these have been reviewed by Bateman (1991):

Recreation

7.16 By far the major recreational use of woodland is for walking and picnics. In the UK the most widely applied technique to obtain a monetary value for this benefit is the 'Travel Cost Method' or TCM (Turner and Bateman, 1990). In this method it is argued that people value woods for recreation at least as much as the costs which they incur to reach them (petrol, car running costs, time, etc.). An average cost of £1.90 per visit 'paid' by visitors to a wood has been calculated by Benson and Willis (1989) from survey data on the distance visitors are prepared to travel, and by what means they travel. To obtain an estimate of the total annual recreation value of a wood this value can be multiplied by annual visitor numbers. Keeble (1991) reports that for one large landfill site in the UK, where community use of parts of the site is encouraged, annual visitor numbers are in the region of 2500.

Amenity value

7.17 Amenity refers to the landscape and general living-environment benefits which woodland can provide. One method of evaluating the monetary value of amenity has been presented by the Arboricultural Association (1990). In this method expert judgement is used to award points to a number of woodland characteristics. For example one category assesses the size of the woodland; a small woodland has a low score and a large woodland a higher score. Similarly, a dense plantation or blatantly derelict area of woodland would be given a low score, and a mature woodland with large trees would be given a high score. The total points score is then multiplied by a conversion factor to obtain the monetary value. Another, more complicated approach is the 'Hedonic Pricing Method' (Garrod and Willis, 1991) which estimates amenity value by comparing the prices of architecturally similar houses near to or far away from the area of the woodland in question. This system of valuation has not yet been fully developed, but it has been shown that the presence of broadleaved woodland near a house can increase its value by up to 7% (Garrod and Willis, 1991).

Wildlife and conservation value

7.18 Little work has been conducted in this country to assess the wildlife and conservation value of forests, but work done in Europe using the 'Contingent Valuation Method' seems to indicate that people would be willing to pay for the creation or conservation of woodland habitats (Bateman, 1991). All the European studies suggest that people value woodland for its wildlife habitat as much as for its recreational benefits.

Carbon fixing

7.19 Carbon dioxide is the main gas responsible for the 'greenhouse effect'. Trees naturally absorb carbon dioxide during growth and convert it into harmless carbon, thus providing a social benefit by contributing to some extent to a reduction in atmospheric carbon dioxide levels. People have used a variety of methods to put a monetary value on this absorption of carbon, and these have often been related to proposed 'carbon taxes'. Another approach has been to use the costs of President Bush's 1990 initiative of planting 1 billion new trees every year to cut net emissions in the US by 5%. The cost of this has been estimated at £25 per ha per year (Bateman, 1991).

Summary and conclusions

7.20 The costs and benefits of establishing woodland on landfill sites should be compared with those of other afteruses as part of the decision-making process associated with landfill restoration. Any cost-benefit analysis may need to take into account social considerations as well as revenue from wood and woodland products, as methods now exist to put a monetary value on social benefits. The main cost of woodland establishment is likely to be that associated with the provision of an adequate depth of rootable soil to ensure long-term tree survival and protection of a clay cap, i.e. 1.5 m. Nevertheless, as trees can be grown in some materials normally considered as waste, it may be possible to obtain revenue for the soil-forming materials used as final cover. The other costs to be taken into consideration are those of planting stock, planting, fencing, weed control, and possibly irrigation and fertilisation.

7.21 Costs may be offset against the benefits of woodland establishment. The Woodland Grant Scheme provides financial assistance for planting and maintenance, and woodland products may provide a financial return as early as 2–3 years after planting (short rotation coppice). The social benefits of woodland, such as recreation, amenity, and conservation value should also be taken into consideration. Methods for evaluating the monetary value of social benefits indicate that they may outweigh the financial costs of woodland establishment in some cases (Willis and Benson, 1989).

Chapter 8

Conclusions

8.1 This report is an evaluation of the potential for woodland establishment on landfill sites. It has been compiled using information from a comprehensive literature review, site visits, and consultations with the minerals industry, mineral planning authorities, waste disposal industry, waste regulation authorities, and specialist scientists involved in landfill and forestry research. It addresses four main areas of concern regarding tree planting on landfill sites, and these are: a) whether trees can successfully be grown on the relatively hostile environment of a landfill site, b) whether tree roots are likely to penetrate through a landfill cap, c) whether tree roots are likely to cause desiccation cracking of a clay cap, and d) whether there is an unacceptable risk of windthrow if trees are planted on landfill sites. The main findings and recommendations resulting from this research are outlined below.

8.2 The advice of Waste Management Paper No. 26 (DoE, 1986) against tree planting on containment landfills has meant that very few landfill sites have been restored to woodland since 1986.

8.3 Despite fears to the contrary, trees can survive and grow well on landfill sites. Nevertheless, poor growth and sometimes outright failure have been quite common, though failure has often been as much a result of factors such as soil compaction, shallow soil, waterlogging and drought, as factors directly related to the landfill, e.g. landfill gas and leachate.

8.4 The majority of tree roots are found within the upper 1 m of soil on undisturbed woodland sites. Most trees have root systems reaching a maximum depth of between 1 and 2 m, though small roots up to 5 m deep have been recorded in the UK. Rooting depth is controlled primarily by soil conditions; vertical development is prevented by unfavourable soil conditions such as compaction and lack of oxygen. Thus, tree roots will not penetrate through HDPE, and are unlikely to penetrate into compacted clay (or other mineral materials) with a bulk density of 1.8 g cm^{-3} or more (recommended minimum density of a clay cap; DoE, 1986) and a very low oxygen concentration. This applies equally well to the taproots of trees, as to any other roots.

8.5 The risk of windthrow needs to be assessed before deciding whether or not to plant trees on landfill sites. A relatively simple assessment of windthrow hazard can be made using the *Windthrow Hazard Classification*. Risk of windthrow can be minimised by encouraging the development of a well-formed root system, through the provision of a sufficient depth of loose soil, by planting trees which are relatively small at maturity, or by managing woodland under the coppice system.

8.6 Tree roots are not considered to be a primary cause of desiccation cracking of a clay cap.

8.7 Closed canopy woodland may help to minimise leachate generation by reducing effective rainfall by up to 20%. The magnitude of this effect is dependent upon how quickly canopy closure is reached. Irrigation of trees with leachate can also help to attenuate its strength and reduce its volume. Irrigation with low strength leachate can stimulate tree growth, but high strength leachate (electrical conductivity of 0.2–0.4 S m^{-1}) is likely to cause injury.

8.8 To protect the cap from damage or desiccation, a suitable depth of soil cover must be provided. For woodland establishment it is recommended that a minimum thickness of 1 m should be provided above an HDPE cap, and 1.5 m above a clay cap.

8.9 It is vitally important that where woodland is to be established on a landfill site soil compaction is avoided. Soil or soil-forming materials should therefore be placed by loose-tipping. If loose-tipping is not possible, or

65

reconsolidation takes place after soil placement, cultivation by deep ripping should be carried out in the season before tree planting.

8.10 Once the cap has been placed it may be prudent to delay tree planting for two or more years to allow for access to sampling boreholes, servicing of pipework and headgear, and any remedial filling which may be required to counteract the effects of differential settlement. If tree planting is to be delayed, it is recommended that planning conditions stipulate that the five year aftercare period (Planning and Compensation Act 1991) does not begin until all the activities necessary to complete the restoration have been undertaken.

8.11 Selection of trees for planting on landfill sites must match species to site conditions. Factors such as susceptibility to windthrow, and tolerance of difficult soil conditions or exposure may need to be considered.

8.12 Suitable planting stock should be used and special attention must be paid to careful plant handling, correct planting procedure and efficient weed control.

8.13 Once established, woodland should be managed so that it achieves its full potential, whether for timber production, landscape enhancement, recreation, wildlife value, or all of these. Poor aftercare management will result in an unsightly and untidy site no matter how good or bad the quality of operations in the restoration phase.

8.14 The financial implications of restoration to woodland should be considered, in particular the cost of providing the recommended thickness (1.5 m) of soil or soil-forming materials on clay-capped sites. However, this must be weighed against the financial returns from sales of timber, and recreational, wildlife and landscape benefits. Many landfill sites will also qualify for grant aid through the Woodland Grant Scheme.

8.15 This study indicates that the potential for woodland establishment on landfill sites is much greater than had previously been thought. Nevertheless, future planting on landfill sites will enable the interactions between tree growth and pollution control measures to be more accurately monitored and evaluated.

8.16 In view of the information presented in this report, it is recommended that guidance contained in Waste Management Paper No. 26 (DoE, 1986), with respect to tree planting on landfill sites, is updated at the earliest opportunity.

References

Ankers, B. and Ruegg, J. (1991). Research into leachate treatment by woodland and grass plot irrigation. Paper presented at Conference 'Discharge Your Obligations'. University of Warwick, Coventry, U.K. 4–5 April, 1991.

Arboricultural Association (1989). Tree roots. Arboricultural Handout No. 6. Arboricultural Association, Romsey.

Arboricultural Association (1990). Amenity valuation of trees and woodlands. Arboricultural Association, Romsey.

Arthur, J.J., Leone, I.A. and Flower, F.B. (1981). Flooding and landfill gas effects on red and sugar maples. *Journal of Environmental Quality* **10**, 431–433.

Bannan, M.W. (1940). The root systems of northern Ontario conifers growing in sand. *American Journal of Botany* **27**, 108–114.

Barbour, J.M.C. (1989). *A study of the use of trees and shrubs as a restoration route for completed landfill sites in Great Britain.* MSc Thesis, Imperial College of Science, Technology and Medicine (University of London).

Bateman, I. (1991). Placing monetary values on the unpriced benefits of forestry. *Quarterly Journal of Forestry* **85**, 152–165.

Bédéneau, M. and Auclair, D. (1989a). The study of tree fine root distribution and dynamics using a combined trench and observation window method. *Annales des Science Forestières* **46**, 283–290.

Bédéneau, M. and Auclair, D. (1989b). Effect of coppicing on hybrid poplar fine root dynamics. *Annales des Sciences Forestières* **46** suppl., 294–296.

Bédéneau, M. and Pages, L. (1984). Study of root rings in coppiced trees. *Annales des Sciences Forestières* **41**, 59–68. (French with English summary.)

Bell, H.J., Dawson, A.R., Baker, C.J. and Wright, C.J. (1991). Tree stability. In, *Research for practical arboriculture.* Ed., S.J. Hodge. Forestry Commission Bulletin 97. HMSO, London, pp.94–101.

Bending, N.A.D. (1991). Site factors affecting tree response on opencast spoils in south Wales. British Coal Corporation Contract. Phase 1 Report. OE/CON/6259. (Unpublished.)

Benson, J. and Willis, K. (1991). The demand for forests for recreation. In, *Forestry expansion: a study of technical, economic and ecological factors.* Paper No 6. Forestry Commission, Edinburgh.

Bibelriether, H. (1962). Research on roots of firs and oaks in middle Swabia. *Forstwissenschaftliches Centralblatt* **81**, 230–247.

Bibelriether, H. (1966). Root development of some tree species in relation to soil properties. *Allgemeine Forst Zeitschrift* **21**, 805–818. Translated from German by the Canadian Department of Forestry and Rural Development. Translation No. 95.

Biddle, P.G. (1983). Patterns of soil drying and moisture deficit in the vicinity of trees on clay soils. *Geotechnique* **33**, 107–126.

Biddle, P.G. (1985). Patterns of soil drying and moisture deficit in the vicinity of trees on clay soils. Research results 1984. Interim Report to Department of Environment. Contract PECD 7/2/014–16/88. (Unpublished.)

Biddle, P.G. (1987). Trees and buildings. In, *Advances in practical arboriculture.* Ed., D. Patch. Forestry Commission Bulletin 65. HMSO, London, pp.121–132.

Biddle, P.G. (1992). Patterns of soil drying and moisture deficit in the vicinity of trees on clay soils. Research results 1991. For Department of Environment, National House-Building Council and Milton Keynes Development Corporation. (Unpublished.)

Binns, W.O. (1979). The hydrological impact of afforestation in Great Britain. In, *Man's impact on the hydrological cycle in the United Kingdom.* Ed., G.E. Hollis. Geo Abstracts, Norwich, pp.55–69.

Binns, W.O. and Fourt, D.F. (1981). Surface workings and trees. In, *Research for practical arboriculture.* Proceedings of the Forestry Commission/Arboricultural Association Seminar at Preston, February 1980, pp.60–75.

Binns, W.O. and Fourt, D.F. (1984). Reclamation of surface workings for trees I. Landforms and cultivation. Arboriculture Research Note 37/84/SSS, Forestry Commission.

Binns, W.O., Mayhead, G.J. and MacKenzie, J.M. (1980). *Nutrient deficiencies of conifers in British forests*. Forestry Commission Leaflet 76. HMSO, London.

Bowen, H.D. (1981). Modifying the root environment to reduce crop stress. *American Society of Agricultural Engineers Monograph* **4**, 21.

Bradshaw, A.D. and Chadwick, M.J. (1980). *The restoration of land*. Blackwell Scientific Publishers, Oxford.

Brennan, G., Patch, D. and Stevens, F.R.W. (1989). Tree roots and underground pipes. Arboriculture Research Note 36/89/TRL. Forestry Commission.

Bronswijk, J.J.B. (1991). Drying, cracking and subsidence of a clay soil in a lysimeter. *Soil Science* **152,** 92–99.

Building Research Establishment (1985). *The influence of trees on house foundations in clay soils*. Building Research Establishment Digest 298.

Building Research Establishment (1989). *The assessment of wind loads Part 3: Wind climate in the United Kingdom*. Building Research Establishment Digest 346.

Büsgen, M. and Münch, E. (1929). *The structure and life of forest trees*. Chapman and Hall Ltd., London. (Translated into English by T. Thomson).

Calder, I.R. and Newson, M.D. (1979). Land-use and upland water resources in Britain – a strategic look. *Water Resources Bulletin* **15**, 1628–1639.

Cheyney, E.G. (1932). The roots of Jack pine. *Journal of Forestry* **30**, 929–932.

Christensen, T.H. and Kjeldsen, P. (1989). Basic biochemical processes in landfills. In, *Sanitary landfilling: process, technology and environmental impact*. Eds., T.H. Christensen, R. Cossu and R. Stegmann. Academic Press, London, pp.29–50.

Coile, T.S. (1951). Review of 'Lasen, L., Lull, N.W. and Frank, B. (1951). Some fundamental plant-soil-water relations in watershed management. USDA Forest Service, Mimeo.' *Journal of Forestry* **49**, 921–923.

Coutts, M.P. (1982). The tolerance of tree roots to waterlogging V. Growth of woody roots of sitka spruce and lodgepole pine in water-logged soil. *New Phytologist* **90**, 467–476.

Coutts, M.P. (1986). Components of tree stability in sitka spruce on peaty gley soil.

Forestry **59**, 173–197.

Croker, T.C. (1958). Soil depth affects windfirmness of longleaf pine. *Journal of Forestry* **56**, 432.

Crossett, R.N. and Campbell, D.J. (1975). The effects of ethylene in the root environment upon the development of barley. *Plant and Soil* **42**, 453–464.

Crossley, D.I. (1940). The effect of a compact subsoil horizon on root penetration. *Journal of Forestry* **38**, 794–796.

Crowther, R.E., Low, A.J. and Tabbush, P.M. (1991). Establishment and tending. In, *Forestry practice*. Ed., B.G. Hibberd. Forestry Commission Handbook 6. HMSO, London, pp.41–80.

Cunningham, I. (1991). Introduction. *Forestry expansion: a study of technical, economic and ecological factors*. Forestry Commission, Edinburgh.

Cureton, P.M., Groenvelt, P.H. and McBride, R.A. (1991). Landfill leachate recirculation: effects on vegetation vigour and clay surface cover infiltration. *Journal of Environmental Quality* **20**, 17–24.

Cutler, D.F. (1991). Tree planting for the future: lessons of the storms of October 1987 and January 1990. *Arboricultural Journal* **15**, 225–234.

Cutler, D.F., Gasson, P.E. and Farmer, M.C. (1990). The wind blown tree survey: analysis of results. *Arboricultural Journal* **14**, 265–286.

Davies, H.L. (1988). Other systems for growing trees on farms. In, *Farm woodland practice*. Ed., B.G. Hibberd. Forestry Commission Handbook 3. HMSO, London, pp.90–101.

Davies, R.J. (1987). *Trees and weeds: weed control for successful tree establishment*. Forestry Commission Handbook 2. HMSO, London.

Day, W.R. (1949). The soil conditions which determine windthrow in forests. *Forestry* **23**, 91–95.

Department of the Environment (1986). *Landfilling wastes*. Waste Management Paper No. 26. HMSO, London.

Department of the Environment (1989). *The reclamation of mineral workings*. Minerals Planning Guidance Note 7. HMSO, London.

Department of the Environment (1990). *Digest of environmental protection and water statistics*. Government Statistical Service Publication No. 13. HMSO, London.

Department of the Environment (1991a). *Survey of land for mineral workings in England 1988. Volume 1 Report on survey results.* HMSO, London.

Department of the Environment (1991b). *The control of landfill gas.* Waste Management Paper No. 27 (2nd Edition). HMSO, London.

Department of the Environment (1992). *A review of options.* Waste Management Paper No. 1 (2nd Edition). HMSO, London.

Dexter, A.R. (1986). Model experiments on the behaviour of roots at the interface between a tilled seed-bed and a compacted sub-soil. I. Effects of seed-bed aggregate size and sub-soil strength on wheat roots. *Plant and Soil* **95,** 123–133.

Dobson, M.C. (1991). *De-icing salt damage to trees and shrubs.* Forestry Commission Bulletin 101. HMSO, London.

Driscoll, R. (1983). The influence of vegetation on the swelling and shrinking of clay in Britain. *Geotechnique* **33**, 93–105.

Ehrig, H.-J. (1989). Leachate quality. In, *Sanitary landfilling: process, technology and environmental impact.* Eds., T.H. Christensen, R. Cossu, and R. Stegmann. Academic Press, London, pp.213–230

Environmental Resources Ltd. (1988). Energy forestry in Britain: environmental issues. Contract report to Department of Energy. Contract No: ETSU B 1166-P1.

Esau, K. (1953). *Plant anatomy.* John Wiley and Sons, New York.

Ettala, M.O. (1988a). Evapotranspiration from a *Salix aquatica* plantation at a sanitary landfill. *Aqua Fennica* **18**, 3–14.

Ettala, M.O. (1988b). Short rotation tree plantations at sanitary landfills. *Waste Management and Research* **6**, 291–302.

Evans, J. (1984). *Silviculture of broadleaved woodland.* Forestry Commission Bulletin 62. HMSO, London.

Faulkner, M.E. and Malcolm, D.C. (1972). Soil physical factors affecting root morphology and stability of Scots pine on upland heaths. *Forestry* **43**, 23–36.

Fayle, D.C.F. (1965). *Rooting habit of sugar maple and yellow birch.* Canadian Department of Forestry Publication No. 1120.

Finch, H. and Bradshaw, A.D. (1990). A soft future for refuse disposal sites. *Landscape Design* June 1990, 36–39.

Flower, F.B., Gilman, E.F. and Leone, I.A. (1981). Landfill gas, what it does to trees and how its injurious effects may be prevented. *Journal of Arboriculture* **7**, 43–52.

Forestry Commission (1990). *Marketing for small woodlands: county lists of mills, merchants and contractors.* HMSO, London.

Forestry Commission (1991). *Community woodland design guidelines.* HMSO, London.

Fraser, A.I. (1962). The soil and roots as factors in tree stability. *Forestry* **35**, 117–127.

Garrod, G.D. and Willis, K.G. (1991). *The hedonic price method and the valuation of countryside characteristics.* Countryside Change Working Paper Series, Paper No. 14. Countryside Change Unit, University of Newcastle.

Gasson, P.E. and Cutler, D.F. (1990). Tree root plate morphology. *Arboricultural Journal* **14,** 193–264.

Gawn, P. (1991). Landscape architecture and gas monitoring techniques. Paper Presented at NAWDC Training Course: Practical Landfill Restoration and Aftercare of Landfill Sites, Crest Hotel, Welwyn Garden City, 18–19 April, 1991.

Gibbs, J.N. and Greig, B.J.W. (1990). Survey of parkland trees after the great storm of October 16, 1987. *Arboricultural Journal* **14**, 321–347.

Gilbert, O.L. (1983). The growth of planted trees subject to fumes from brickworks. *Environmental Pollution* (Series A) **31**, 301–310.

Gilbertson, P., Kendle, A.D. and Bradshaw, A.D. (1987). Root growth and the problems of trees in urban and industrial areas. In, *Advances in practical arboriculture.* Ed., D. Patch. HMSO, London, pp.59–66.

Gill, W.R. and Bolt, G.H. (1955). Pfeffer's studies of the root growth pressures exerted by plants. *Agronomy Journal* **47**, 161–168.

Gilman, E.F., Flower, F.B. and Leone, I.A. (1985). Standardized procedures for planting vegetation on completed sanitary landfills. *Waste Management and Research* **3**, 65–80.

Gilman, E.F., Leone, I.A. and Flower, F.B. (1981). The adaptability of 19 woody species in vegetating a former sanitary landfill. *Forest Science* **27**, 13–18.

Gilman, E.F., Leone, I.A. and Flower, F.B. (1982). Influence of soil gas contamination on tree root growth. *Plant and Soil* **65**, 3–10.

Gordon, A.M., McBride, R.A. and Fisken, A.J. (1989). Effect of landfill leachate irrigation on red maple (*Acer rubrum* L.) and sugar maple (*Acer saccharum* Marsh.) seedling growth and on foliar nutrient concentrations. *Environmental Pollution* **56**, 327–336.

Graves, W.R., Joly, R.J. and Dana, M.N. (1991). Water use and growth of honeylocust and tree of heaven at high root-zone temperature. *Hortscience* **26**, 1309–1312.

Grayson, A.J. (Ed.). (1989). *The 1987 storm: impacts and responses.* Forestry Commission Bulletin 87. HMSO, London.

Greacen, E.L. (1986). Root response to soil mechanical properties. Transactions of the 13th congress of the International Society of Soil Science, Hamburg, pp.20–47.

Greacen, E.L. and Sands, R. (1980). Composition of forest soils – a review. *Australian Journal of Soil Research* **8**, 163–189.

Greene-Kelly, R. (1974). Shrinkage of clay soils: a statistical correlation with other soil properties. *Geoderma* **11**, 243–257.

Grefe, R.P., Heubner, P.M. and Gordon, M.E. (1987). Multi-layered cover design and application to Wisconson landfills. 18th Annual Madison Waste Conference, 29–30 September. University of Wisconsin, Madison, USA.

Gregory, P.J. (1988). Water and crop growth. In, *Russell's soil conditions and plant growth.* Ed., A. Wild. Longman Scientific and Technical, Harlow, Essex, pp.338–377.

Greig, D.A. and Thompson, D.A. (1991). Marketing and utilisation. In, *Forestry practice.* Ed., B.G. Hibberd. HMSO, London, pp.187–196.

Haines, W.B. (1923). The volume changes associated with variations of water content in the soil. *Journal of Agricultural Science,* Cambridge **13**, 296–310.

Hall, R.L. and Roberts, J.M. (1989). Hydrological aspects of new broadleaf plantations. *Seesoil* **6**, 2–38.

Harley, J.L. (1940). A study of the root system of the beech in woodland soil with especial reference to mycorrhizal infection. *Journal of Ecology* **28**, 107–117.

Hayward, N.P. (1991). Report of a visit to Elsenham Quarry, June 1991. Unpublished Forestry Commission Internal Report.

Heilman, P. (1981). Root penetration of Douglas-fir seedlings into compacted soil. *Forest Science* **27**, 660–666.

Hoeks, J. (1983). Significance of biogas production in waste tips. *Waste Management and Research* **1**, 323–325.

Houghton, J.T., Jenkins, G.J. and Ephraums, J.J. (Eds.). (1990). *Climate change: the IPCC scientific assessment.* Cambridge University Press, Cambridge.

Hudson, J.A. (1988). The contribution of soil moisture storage to the water balances of upland forested and grassland catchments. *Hydrological Sciences Journal* **33**, 289–309.

Hutte, P. (1968). Experiments on windflow and wind damage in Germany; site and susceptibility of spruce forests to storm damage. In, Supplement to *Forestry*; *Wind effects on the forest*, 20–26.

Insley, H. (1980). Wasting trees? – The effects of handling and post planting maintenance on the survival and growth of amenity trees. *Arboricultural Journal* **4**, 65–73.

Interdepartmental Committee on the Redevelopment of Contaminated Land (1987). *Guidance on the assessment and redevelopment of contaminated land.* ICRCL Guidance Note 59/83. Department of the Environment.

Harding, R.J., Hall, R.L., Neal, C., Roberts, J.M., Rosier, P.T.W. and Kinniburgh, D.G. (1992). *Hydrological impacts of broadleaf woodlands: implications for water use and water quality.* National Rivers Authority.

Jacobson, J. and Clyde-Hill, A. (Eds.). (1970). *Recognition of air pollution injury to vegetation.* Air Pollution Control Association, Pittsburgh, Pennsylvania.

Kappeli, T. and Shulin, R. (1988). Lysimeter studies on the water balance of poplar, *Alnus incana, Picea abies* and grass on a sandy soil over gravel. *Schweizerische Zeitschrift fur Forstwesen* **139**, 129–143. (In German).

Karizumi, N. (1957). *Studies on the form and distribution habit of the tree root.* Bulletin of the Government Forest Experiment Station No. 94. Tokyo, Japan.

Keeble, R. (1991). Land use and planning issues. Paper Presented at NAWDC Training Course: Practical Landfill Restoration and Aftercare of Landfill Sites, Crest Hotel, Welwyn Garden City, 18–19 April, 1991.

Kirby, C., Newson, M.D. and Gilman, K. (Eds.). (1991). *Plynlimon research: the first two decades.* Institute of Hydrology Report No. 109. IOH, Wallingford.

Knox, K. (1989). Practice and trends in landfill in the U.K. In, *Sanitary landfilling: process technology and environmental impact.* Eds., T.H. Christensen, R. Cossu and R. Stegmann. Academic Press, London, pp.533–548.

Knox, K. (1991a). Water management at landfills: water balance and practical aspects. Notes to accompany lecture at NAWDC course held at Meriden, Coventry, 8 May 1991.

Knox, K. (1991b). A review of water balance methods and their application to landfill in the UK. Report CWM 031/91 prepared for the UK Department of the Environment under Contract No. PECD 7/10/236.

Kochenderfer, J.N. (1973). Root distribution under some forest types native to West Virginia. *Ecology* **54**, 445–448.

Köstler, J.N., Brückner, E. and Bibelriether, H. (1968). *Die Wurzeln der Waldbaum.* Verlag Paul Parey, Hamburg.

Kozlowski, T.T. (1986). Soil aeration and growth of forest trees. *Scandinavian Journal of Forest Research* **1**, 113–123.

Kozlowski, T.T. (1991). Soil aeration, compaction and flooding. In, *The physiological ecology of woody plants.* Eds., T.T. Kozlowski, P.J. Kramer and S.G. Pallardy. Academic Press, San Diego, pp.303–337.

Kreutzer, K. (1961). Root development of young forest trees on pseudo-gley soils. *Forstwissenschaftliches Centralblatt* **80**, 356–392. (In German).

Laing, E.V. (1932). *Studies on tree roots.* Forestry Commission Bulletin 13, HMSO, London.

Laitakari, E. (1929). The root system of pine (*Pinus sylvestris*). A morphological investigation. *Acta Forestalia Fennica* **33**, 1–306 (Finnish), 307–380 (English summary).

Laitakari, E. (1935). The root system of birch (*Betula verrucosa* and *odorata*). *Acta Forestalia Fennica* **41**, 1–168 (Finnish), 169–216 (English summary).

Larkin, M. (1990). *A comparison of restored landfill sites in Bedfordshire.* MSc Thesis. Department of Land and Water Management, Silsoe College, Cranfield.

Larsson, S. (1981). Influence of intercepted water on transpiration and evaporation of *Salix. Agricultural Meteorology* **23**, 331–338.

Law, F. (1956). The effect of afforestation upon the yield of water catchment areas. *Journal of the British Waterworks Association* **38**, 484–494.

Leach, A. and Moss, H.D.T. (1989). Landfill gas research and development studies: Calvert and Stewartby landfill sites. Contract report to Department of Energy. Contract No. ETSU B 1164.

Lechner, P. (1989). The Austrian guidelines for sanitary landfills. In, *Sanitary landfilling: process technology and environmental impact.* Eds., T.H. Christensen, R. Cossu and R. Stegmann. Academic Press, London, pp.523–532.

Leone, I.A., Flower, F.B., Arthur, J.J. and Gilman, E.F. (1977). Damage to woody species by anaerobic landfill gases. *Journal of Arboriculture* **3**, 221–225.

Leone, I.A., Flower, F.B., Gilman, E.F. and Arthur, J.J. (1979). Adapting woody species and planting techniques to landfill conditions: field and laboratory investigations. US EPA Report 600/2–79–128.

Leone, I.A., Gilman, E.F. and Flower, F.B. (1982). Growing trees on completed sanitary landfills. *Arboricultural Journal* **7**, 247–252.

Leyton, L. (1956). Aeration and root growth in tree seedlings. 12th Congress of the International Union of Forest Research Organisations. No 56/21/5, pp.123–126.

Linder, S. (1985). Potential and actual production in Australian forest stands. In, *Research for forest management.* Eds., J.J. Landsberg and W. Parsons. CSIRO, Melbourne, pp.11–35.

Lutz, H.J., Ely, J.B. and Little, S. (1937). *The influence of soil profile horizons on root distribution of white pine* (Pinus strobus). Yale University School of Forestry Bulletin No. 44.

Lyford, W.H. (1975). Rhizography of non-woody roots of trees in the forest floor. In, *Development and function of roots.* Eds., J.G. Torrey and D.T. Clarkson. Academic Press, London, pp. 179–196.

Lyford, W.H. and Wilson, B.F. (1964). *Development of the root system of* Acer rubrum L. Harvard Forest Paper No. 10.

Lyr, H. and Hoffmann, G. (1967). Growth rates and growth periodicity of tree roots. *International Review of Forest Research* **2**, 181–236.

McMinn, R.G. (1963). Characteristics of Douglas-fir root systems. *Canadian Journal of Botany* **41**, 105–122.

Maitland, P.S., Newson, M.D. and Best, G.A. (1990). *The impact of afforestation and forestry practice on freshwater habitats*. Focus on Nature Conservation No. 23. Nature Conservancy Council, Peterborough.

Mayer, H. (1989). Windthrow. *Philosophical Transactions of the Royal Society of London* (Series B) **324**, 267–281.

Menser, H.A., Winant, W.M. and Bennett, O.L. (1983). Spray irrigation with landfill leachate. *BioCycle* **24**, 22–25.

Miller, K.F. (1985). *Windthrow hazard classification*. Forestry Commission Leaflet 85. HMSO, London.

Minore, D., Smith, C.E. and Woolard, R.F. (1969). *Effects of high soil density on seedling root growth of seven northwestern tree species*. USDA Forest Service Research Note PNW–112.

Mitchell, A.F. (1981). The native and exotic trees in Britain. Arboriculture Research Note 29/81/SILS, Forestry Commission.

Moffat, A.J. (1988). Sewage sludge as a fertiliser in amenity and reclamation plantings. Arboriculture Research Note 76/88/SSS, Forestry Commission.

Moffat, A.J. (1989). The new site. In, *Urban forestry practice*. Ed., B.G. Hibberd. Forestry Commission Handbook 5. HMSO, London, pp.40–47.

Moffat, A.J. (1991). Practical use of sites – forestry. Paper Presented at NAWDC Training Course: Practical Landfill Restoration and Aftercare of Landfill Sites, Crest Hotel, Welwyn Garden City, 18–19 April, 1991.

Moffat, A.J. (in press). Site related aspects of short rotation coppice. In, *Short rotation coppice*. Ed., P.M. Tabbush. Forestry Commission Bulletin. HMSO, London.

Moffat, A.J. and Bending, N.A.D. (1992). *Physical site evaluation for community woodland establishment*. Research Information Note 216. Forestry Commission, Edinburgh.

Moffat, A.J. and Houston, T.J. (1991). Tree establishment and growth at Pitsea landfill site, Essex, U.K. *Waste Management and Research* **9**, 35–46.

Moffat, A.J. and McNeill, J.D. (in press). *The reclamation of mineral workings and other disturbed land for forestry*. Forestry Commission Bulletin. HMSO, London.

Mullins, C.E. (1991). Physical properties of soils in urban areas. In, *Soils in the urban environment*. Eds., P. Bullock and P.J. Gregory. Blackwell Scientific Publications, Oxford, pp.87–118.

National Audit Office (1986). *Review of the Forestry Commission's objectives and achievements*. Report by the Comptroller and Auditor General. HMSO, London.

National Rivers Authority (1991). *Policy and practice for the protection of groundwater*. Draft Consultation Document. Nov 1991.

Neal, C., Robson, R.L., Hall, G., Ryland, T., Conway, T. and Neal, M. (1991). Hydrological impacts of hardwood plantation in lowland Britain: preliminary findings on interception at a forest edge, Black Wood, Hampshire, southern England. *Journal of Hydrology* **127**, 349–365.

Norfalaise, A. (1959). Sur l'interception de la pluie par le couvert dans quelques fôrets belges. *Bulletin de la Sociéte Royale Forestière de la Belgique* **10**, 433–439.

Pan, E. and Bassuk, N. (1985). Effects of soil type and compaction on the growth of *Ailanthus altissima* seedlings. *Journal of Environmental Horticulture* **3**, 158–162.

Pankhurst, E.S. (1980). The effects of natural gas on trees and other vegetation. *Techniques* **35**, 32–33. British Gas.

Pepper, H.W. (1992). *Forest fencing*. Forestry Commission Bulletin 102. HMSO, London.

Perry, T.O. (1982). The ecology of tree roots and the practical significance thereof. *Journal of Arboriculture* **8**, 197–211.

Perry, T.O. (1989). Tree roots: facts and fallacies. *Arnoldia* **49**, 1–21.

Pfeffer, W. (1893). Druck und Arbeitsliestung durch Wachsende Pflanzen. *Abhandlungen der Koniglich Sachsischen Gesellschaft der Wissenschaften* **33**, 235–474.

Potter, C.J. (1989). Establishment and early maintenance. In, *Urban forestry practice*. Ed., B.G. Hibberd. Forestry Commission Handbook 5. HMSO, London, pp. 78–90.

Potter, C.J. (1990). Coppiced trees as energy crops. Contract Report to the Department of Energy. Contract No. ETSU B 1078.

Potter, M.J. (1991). *Treeshelters*. Forestry Commission Handbook 7. HMSO, London.

Pyatt, D.G. (1977). *Guide to site-types in forests of north and mid Wales*. Forestry Commission Forest Record 69. HMSO, London.

Quine, C.P. (1991). Recent storm damage to trees and woodlands in southern Britain. In, *Research for practical arboriculture*. Ed., S.J. Hodge. Forestry Commission Bulletin 97. HMSO, London, pp.83–89.

Quine, C.P. and Reynard, B.R. (1990). *A new series of windthrow monitoring areas in upland Britain*. Forestry Commission Occasional Paper 25. Forestry Commission, Edinburgh.

Quine, C.P., Burnand, A.C., Coutts, M.P. and Reynard, B.R. (1991). Effects of mounds and stumps on the root architecture of sitka spruce on a peaty gley restocking site. *Forestry* **64**, 385–401.

Rajappan, J. and Boynton, C.E. (1956). Responses of red and black raspberry root systems to differences in O_2 and CO_2, pressures and temperatures. *Proceedings of the American Society of Horticultural Science* **75**, 402–500.

Reeve, M. (1991). Soil handling and restoration materials. Paper Presented at NAWDC Training Course: Practical Landfill Restoration and Aftercare of Landfill Sites, Crest Hotel, Welwyn Garden City, 18–19 April, 1991.

Reeve, M.J. and Hall, D.G.M. (1978). Shrinkage in clayey subsoils of contrasting structure. *Journal of Soil Science* **29**, 315–323.

Reeve, M.J., Hall, D.G.M. and Bullock, P. (1980). The effect of soil composition and environmental factors on the shrinkage of some clayey British soils. *Journal of Soil Science* **31**, 429–442.

Reeve, M.J., Smith, P.D. and Thomasson, A.J. (1973). The effect of density on water retention properties of field soils. *Journal of Soil Science* **24**, 355–367.

Richards, D. and Cockcroft, B. (1974). Soil physical properties and root concentrations in an irrigated apple orchard. *Australian Journal of Experimental Agriculture and Animal Husbandry* **14**, 103–107.

RMC (1987). *A practical guide to restoration*. RMC Group plc, Feltham, Middlesex.

Roberts, J. (1983). Forest transpiration: a conservative hydrological process? *Journal of Hydrology* **66**, 133–141.

Robinson, H.D. (1991). Groundwater protection in the UK – assessment of the landfill leachate source-term. Annual Symposium of the Institution of Water and Environmental Management, Groundwater Pollution and Aquifer Protection in Europe. 8–9 Oct 1991, Palais des Congres, Paris, France.

Röhrig, R. (1966). Root development of forest trees in relation to ecological conditions. Part I and II. *Forstarchiv* **37**, 217–229 and 237–249. Translated from German by the Canadian Department of Forestry and Rural Development. Translation No. 101.

Romberger, J.A. (1963). *Meristems, growth and development in woody plants*. USDA Forest Service, Technical Bulletin 1293.

Ruark, G.A., Mader, D.L. and Tattar, T.A. (1982). The influence of soil compaction and aeration on the root growth and vigour of trees – a literature review. Part I. *Arboricultural Journal* **6**, 251–265.

Ruark, G.A., Mader, D.L. and Tattar, T.A. (1983). The influence of soil moisture and temperature on the root growth and vigour of trees – a literature review. Part II. *Arboricultural Journal* **7**, 39–51.

Rutter, A.J. (1962). Estimating transpiration and evaporation from forests. *Pakistan Journal of Forestry* **12**, 115–123.

Rutter, A.J. and Fourt, D.F. (1965). Studies in the water relations of *Pinus sylvestris* in plantation conditions III. A comparison of soil water changes and estimates of total evaporation on four afforested sites and one grass-covered site. *Journal of Applied Ecology* **2**, 197–209.

Schaetzl, R.J., Johnson, D.L., Burns, S.F. and Small, T.W. (1989). Tree uprooting: review of terminology, process, and environmental implications. *Canadian Journal of Forest Research* **19**, 1–11.

Schuster, C.E. (1936). Root development of trees as affected by physical properties of the soils. *Proceedings of the Washington State Horticultural Association* **32**, 22–26.

Scott-Russell, R. (1977). *Plant root systems: their function and interaction with the soil*. McGraw Hill Book Co., Maidenhead, Berkshire.

Scully, N.J. (1942). Root distribution and environment in a maple-oak forest. *Botanical Gazette* **103**, 492–517.

Sheely, J.E. and Cooper, J.P. (1973). Light interception, photosynthetic activity and crop growth rate in canopies of six temperate forage grasses. *Journal of Applied Ecology* **10**, 235–250.

Shoulders, E. and Ralston, C.W. (1975). Temperature, root aeration, and light influence slash pine nutrient uptake rates. *Forest Science* **21**, 401–410.

Smith, K.A. and Dowdell, R.J. (1974). Field studies of the soil atmosphere I. Relationships between ethylene, oxygen and soil moisture content and temperature. *Journal of Soil Science* **25**, 217–230.

Stief, K. (1989). Multi-barrier concept in West Germany. In, *Sanitary landfilling: process technology and environmental impact*. Eds., T.H. Christensen, R. Cossu and R. Stegmann. Academic Press, London, pp.559–576.

Stout, B.B. (1956). *Studies of the root systems of deciduous trees*. Black Rock Forest Bulletin 15. New York.

Sutton, R.F. (1969). *Form and development of conifer root systems*. Commonwealth Agricultural Bureau Technical Communication No.7.

Sutton, R.F. (1980). Root system morphogenesis. *New Zealand Journal of Forest Science* **10**, 265–292.

Tattar, T.A. (1978). *Diseases of shade trees*. Academic Press, London.

Taylor, H.M. and Brar, G.S. (1991). Effect of soil compaction on root development. *Soil and Tillage Research* **19**, 111–119.

Taylor, H.M. and Gardner, H.R. (1960). Relative penetrating ability of different plant roots. *Agronomy Journal* **52**, 579–581.

Taylor, H.M. and Ratliff, L.F. (1969). Root growth pressures of cotton, peas, and peanuts. *Agronomy Journal* **61**, 398–402.

Thompson, F.B. (1972). Rainfall interception by oak coppice (*Quercus robur* L.). In, *Research papers in forest meteorology, an Aberystwyth symposium*. Ed., J.A. Taylor. The Cambrian News Ltd., pp.59–74.

Toumey, J.W. (1929). Initial root habit in American trees and its bearing on regeneration. *International Congress of Plant Science Proceedings* **1**, 713–728.

Trousdell, K.B., Williams, W.C. and Nelson, T.C. (1965). Damage to recently thinned loblolly pine stands by Hurricane Donna. *Journal of Forestry* **63**, 95–100.

Trouse, A.C. (1971). Soil conditions as they affect plant establishment, root development and yield: Effects of soil temperature on plant activities. In, *Compaction of Agricultural Soils*. American Society of Agricultural Engineers Monograph, pp.269–312.

Turner, R.K. and Bateman, I.J. (1990). *A critical review of monetary assessement methods and techniques*. Environmental Assessment Group, University of East Anglia.

Vater, H. (1927). The root system of pine, spruce and beech. USDA Forest Service Translation No 301. (Translated by A.H. Krappe from *Tharandter Forstliches Jarbuch* **78**, 65–85).

Ward, R.C. (1975). *Principles of hydrology*. McGraw-Hill Book Company (UK) Ltd., London.

Warkentin, B.P. (1971). Effects of compaction on content and transmission of water in soils. In, *Compaction of agricultural soils*. American Society of Agricultural Engineers Monograph, pp.126–153.

Wiersum, L.K. (1957). The relationship of the size and structural rigidity of pores to their penetration by roots. *Plant and Soil* **9**, 75–85.

Williamson, D.R. and Lane, P.B. (1989). *The use of herbicides in the forest*. Forestry Commission Field Book 8. HMSO, London.

Williamson, D.R. and Mason, W.L. (1991). Nursery practice. In, *Forestry practice*. Ed., B.G. Hibberd. Forestry Commission Handbook 6. HMSO, London, pp.17–24.

Willis, K.G. and Benson, J.F. (1989). Recreational values of forests. *Forestry* **62**, 93–110.

Wilson, G. (1991). Post closure problems on landfill sites. Paper Presented at NAWDC Training Course: Practical Landfill Restoration and Aftercare of Landfill Sites, Crest Hotel, Welwyn Garden City, 18–19 April, 1991.

Wilson, K. (1985). *A guide to reclamation of mineral workings for forestry*. Forestry Commission Research and Development Paper 141. Forestry Commission, Edinburgh.

Wilson, K. (1987). Reclamation of mineral workings to forestry. In, *Advances in practical arboriculture*. Ed., D. Patch. Forestry Commission Bulletin 65, HMSO, London, pp.38–41.

Wolstenholme, R., Dutch, J., Moffat, A.J., Bayes, C.D. and Taylor, C.M.A. (1992). *A manual of good practice for the use of sewage sludge in forestry*. Forestry Commission Bulletin 107. HMSO, London.

Wong, M.H. and Leung, C.K. (1989). Landfill leachate as irrigation water for tree and vegetable crops. *Waste Management and Research* **7**, 311–324.

Yeager, A.F. (1935). Root systems of certain trees and shrubs growing on prairie soils. *Journal of Agricultural Research* **51**, 1085–1092.

Yeatman, C.W. (1955). *Tree root development on upland heaths*. Forestry Commission Bulletin 21. HMSO, London.

Yelenosky, G. (1964). Tolerance of trees to deficiencies of soil aeration. *Proceedings of the International Shade Tree Conference* **40**, 127–148.

Yule, D.F. and Ritchie, J.T. (1980). Soil shrinkage relationships of Texas vertisols II. Large cores. *Soil Science Society of America Journal* **44**, 1291–1295.

Zahner, R. (1968). Water deficits and growth of trees. In, *Water deficits and plant growth Vol II: plant water consumption and response*. Ed., T.T. Kozlowski. Academic Press, London, pp.191–254.

Zisa, R.P., Halverson, H.G. and Stout, B.J. (1980). *Establishment and early growth of conifers on compact soils in urban areas*. USDA Forest Service Research Paper NE 451.

Appendix 1

Details of tree performance on 19 restored landfill sites

Site details	Soil, capping: depth and type	Planting date	Tree Species	Performance	Additional information
Lottbridge Drove Eastbourne, East Sussex. Operational Grid ref: TQ615016	0–20 cm silty clay loam 20–40 cm silty clay 40–100 cm grey silty clay No engineered low permeability cap	1983	Ash Field maple Turkey oak White poplar English oak Goat willow Grey alder Swedish whitebeam White willow Corsican pine Hornbeam Small-leafed lime Sycamore	Good Moderate Poor	1. Size of site: 30 ha. 2. Landform: domed. 3. Tree coverage 5%. 4. Location of trees: block on edge slope. 5. Stock type: whips or transplants. 6. Tree shelters: none. 7. Weed control: for first few years. 8. Root depth: not assessed. 9. Methane: none detected. 10. Landscape value: good. 11. Other: Annual assessments of tree health carried out by Brighton Polytechnic.
Mountfield tip (new) Battle, East Sussex. Operational Grid ref: TQ746195	No soil cover >1 m clay (cap?)	1990	Grey alder Ash English oak Field maple Birch Hazel Holly	Good Moderate Poor	1. Size of site: 5 ha. 2. Landform: domed. 3. Tree coverage: 10%. 4. Location of trees: edge slope. 5. Stock type: whips. 6. Tree shelters: for 50% of trees. 7. Weed control: not necessary at present. 8. Root depth: not assessed. 9. Methane: none detected. 10. Landscape value: too early to assess. 11. Other: Trees planted directly into clay cap.
Mountfield tip (old) Battle, East Sussex. Closed (c 1965) Grid ref: TQ743194	1 cm litter >1 m compact sandy silt loam No horizons detected No low permeability cap	1966	Scots pine	Good	1. Size of site: 5 ha. 2. Landform: flat. 3. Tree coverage: 100%. 4. Location of trees: whole site. 5. Stock type: 1 + 1 transplants. 6. Tree shelters: not invented in 1966.

Site details	Soil capping: depth and type	Planting date	Tree species	Performance	Additional information
					7. Weed control: not known.
					8. Root depth: not assessed.
					9. Methane: none detected.
					10. Landscape value: excellent.
					11. Other: Average height of trees in 1977–1.82 m. Average height in 1991–8 m.
Somerley tip Ringwood, Hampshire. Operational Grid ref: SU070121 Phase 1	0.8–1.2 m sandy loam Front detected at about 0.3–0.6 m below which soil changed from orchreous to grey/green in colour High methane concentrations detected in lower layer No low permeability cap	1982	Bishop pine Common alder Corsican pine Monterey pine Red alder Scots pine (self sown) Japanese larch	Good Moderate – poor	1. Size of site: 5 ha. 2. Landform: sloping with 2 x 90 m ridges. 3. Tree coverage: 90%. 4. Location of trees: whole site. 5. Stock type: 1 + 1 transplants. 6. Tree shelters: not used. 7. Weed control: for first 3 years. 8. Root depth: Max 0.58 m. Average 0 .42 m. 9. Methane: 50% at 1 m. 10. Landscape value: good. 11. Other: Tree roots only in upper aerobic layer of soil.
Somerley tip Ringwood, Hampshire. Operational Grid ref: SU070121 Phase 2	As above	1989	Birch Common alder English oak Goat willow Ash Crack willow Dog rose Guelder rose Flowering crab Hawthorn Larch Rowan	Moderate Poor	1. Size of site: 5 ha. 2. Landform: two 90 m x 1.5 m ridges. 3. Tree coverage: 90%. 4. Location of trees: whole site. 5. Stock type: 1 + 1 transplants. 6. Tree shelters: not used. 7. Weed control: herbicide. 8. Root depth: not assessed. 9. Methane: not assessed. 10. Landscape value of trees: poor. 11. Other: Planting characterised by repeated dieback and regrowth.

Site details	Soil, capping: depth and type	Planting date	Tree species	Performance	Additional information
West Wood, Netley, Hampshire. Closed (c 1989) Grid ref: SU452095	Stony, silty loam; unknown depth Uncertain as to presence of cap	1990	Birch English oak Holly Ash Common alder White willow Beech Red oak Rowan	Good Moderate Poor	1. Size of site: 5 ha. 2. Landform: domed. 3. Tree coverage: 20%. 4. Location of trees: edge slopes. 5. Stock type: whips and transplants. 6. Tree shelters: for 15% of trees. 7. Weed control: herbicide. 8. Root depth: not assessed. 9. Methane: not assessed. 10. Landscape value: too early to assess. 11. Other: Methane 'hot spots' in evidence.
Henlow, Bedfordshire. Closed (c 1970) Grid ref: TL178400	>50 cm loose, fine sandy loam (pH 6.7–7.6). Unknown depth of subsoil No low permeability cap	1980	Corsican pine Dog rose English oak Hawthorn Norway maple Scots pine (self sown) Grey alder	Good Poor	1. Size of site: 6 ha. 2. Landform: flat. 3. Tree coverage: 50% 4. Location of trees: one half of site. 5. Stock type: whips. 6. Tree shelters: not used. 7. Weed control: for first five years. 8. Root depth: not assessed. 9. Methane: none detected. 10. Landscape value: excellent. 11. Other: Site evaluated in Larkin (1990).
Holme Green, Bedfordshire. Closed (c 1970) Grid ref: TL197428	20 cm fine sandy loam Unknown depth of subsoil No low permeability cap	1981 and 1983	Cherry English oak European larch Grey alder Italian alder Norway maple Corsican pine	Good Failed	1. Size of site: 2 ha. 2. Landform: flat. 3. Tree coverage: 95%. 4. Location of trees: whole site. 5. Stock type: whips. 6. Tree shelters: not used. 7. Weed control: for first five years. 8. Root depth: not assessed. 9. Methane: none detected. 10. Landscape value: excellent. 11. Other:

Site details	Soil, capping: depth and type	Planting date	Tree species	Performance	Additional information
Sundon, Bedfordshire. Operational Grid ref: TL035289	>1 m chalky subsoil Presence of cap unknown	1986 and 1989	Italian alder Cherry Ash Field maple Sycamore	Good Moderate	1. Size of site: 20 ha. 2. Landform: domed. 3. Tree coverage: 10%. 4. Location of trees: edge slope. 5. Stock type: whips. 6. Tree shelters: not used. 7. Weed control: herbicide. 8. Root depth: not assessed. 9. Methane: none detected. 10. Landscape value: too early to assess. 11. Other:
Blue Waters, Houghton Regis, Bedfordshire. Closed (c 1979) Grid ref: TL013245	Approx. 1 m compact chalky/flinty subsoil pH 7.3–7.8 No low permeability cap	1981	Dog rose (self sown) Field maple Italian alder Norway maple Ash Austrian pine Cherry Hornbeam Lime	Good Poor	1. Size of site: 4.7 ha. 2. Landform: slope. 3. Tree coverage: 95%. 4. Location of trees: whole site. 5. Stock type: transplants. 6. Tree shelters: not used. 7. Weed control: herbicide. 8. Root depth: not assessed. 9. Methane: none detected. 10. Landscape value: moderate-poor. 11. Other: High soil pH and weed competition were obviously restricting growth.
Beeston tip, Leeds, West Yorkshire. Closed (c 1970) Grid ref: SE288315	0–15 cm sandy silt loam 15–45 cm subsoil No low permeability cap	1974 and 1977	Birch Cherry Common alder Elder Horse chestnut False acacia Swedish whitebeam Sycamore Willow	Good	1. Size of site: 3 ha. 2. Landform: steep slope. 3. Tree coverage: 50%. 4. Location of trees: bottom of slope. 5. Stock type: transplants. 6. Tree shelters: not invented in 1974. 7. Weed control: not known. 8. Root depth: not assessed. 9. Methane: none detected.

Site details	Soil, capping: depth and type	Planting date	Tree species	Performance	Additional information
			Grey alder Hornbeam	Moderate	10. Landscape value: excellent. 11. Other: Growth tended to be better at the bottom of the slope.
Westwood, Leeds, West Yorkshire. Closed (c 1978) Grid ref: SE287313	30–50 cm of subsoil No low permeability cap	1983	Birch Turkey oak Italian alder Sycamore Beech Lodgepole pine Swedish whitebeam Sycamore Willow	Good Moderate Poor	1. Size of site: 20 ha. 2. Landform: plateau and steep slope. 3. Tree coverage: 50%. 4. Location of trees: edge slope. 5. Stock type: transplants. 6. Tree shelters: not used. 7. Weed control: for first 5 years. 8. Root depth: not assessed. 9. Methane: none detected. 10. Landscape value: moderate. 11. Other: Some of the patchiness in growth was due to a fire.
Beeston Royds, Leeds, West Yorkshire. Closed (c 1988) Grid ref: SE267313	0–30 cm subsoil, unknown depth of inert material below subsoil No low permeability cap	1989	English oak Grey alder Beech Birch	Moderate Poor	1. Size of site 5 ha. 2. Landform: sloping hillside. 3. Tree coverage: 30%. 4. Location of trees: various, in groups. 5. Stock type: transplants. 6. Tree shelters: not used. 7. Weed control: herbicide granules. 8. Root depth: not assessed. 9. Methane: not assessed. 10. Landscape value: too early to assess. 11. Other: Vigorous competition from weeds, especially clover, thus poor growth.
Birchencliffe, Leeds, West Yorkshire. Closed (c 1975)	Approximately 1 m of weathered colliery shale No low permeability cap	1977	Ash Birch Hornbeam Horse chestnut Swedish whitebeam	Good	1. Size of site: 2 ha. 2. Landform: slightly domed. 3. Tree coverage: 90% 4. Location of trees: whole site.

Site details	Soil, capping: depth and type	Planting date	Tree species	Performance	Additional information
Grid ref: SE117185			Sycamore		5. Stock type: transplants 6. Tree shelters: not used. 7. Weed control: not known. 8. Root depth: not assessed. 9. Methane: not assessed. 10. Landscape value: excellent. 11. Other: Tree growth generally good but evidence of premature decline.
Horbury Lagoons, Leeds, West Yorkshire. Closed (c 1972) Grid ref: SE307175	Unknown depth of soil No low permeability cap cap	1975	Corsican pine Goat willow False acacia White poplar	Good	1. Size of site: 10 ha. 2. Landform: flat. 3. Tree coverage: 15%. 4. Location of trees: in groups 5. Stock type: not known. 6. Tree shelters: not used. 7. Weed control: not known. 8. Root depth: not assessed. 9. Methane: not assessed. 10. Landscape value: excellent. 11. Other: Multi-purpose site with lake, grassland and areas of woodland.
Nab Lane, Wakefield, West Yorkshire. Closed (c 1989) Grid ref: SE237273	0–30 cm sandy subsoil 30–50 cm brick waste 50–100 cm colliery spoil No low permeability cap	1982	Turkey oak Common alder Italian alder Sycamore	Good Moderate	1. Size of site: 5 ha. 2. Landform: slightly sloping. 3. Tree coverge: 20%. 4. Location of trees: in blocks. 5. Stock type: whips or transplants. 6. Tree shelters: not used. 7. Weed control: for first 5 years. 8. Root depth: maximum 0.5 m, average 0.36 m. 9. Methane: none detected.

Site details	Soil, capping: depth and type	Planting date	Tree species	Performance	Additional information
					10. Landscape value: moderate.
					11. Other: Root growth tended to stop at brick rubble.
Corby, Northamptonshire. Operational Grid ref: SP878909	Restoration in 5 phases: Phase 1; no cap, 30 cm of compact silty clay loam. Phase 2; no cap, 70 cm high ridges of compact soil. Phase 3; flat, compact soil over clay cap. Phase 4; covered with 1 m clay and 1-2 m topsoil. No trees Phase 5; still being filled	1983 1986 1989	Ash English oak Field maple Grey alder Hawthorn Italian alder Lime Red alder Sycamore	Poor	1. Size of site: 10 ha. 2. Landform: mostly flat. 3. Tree coverage: 70%. 4. Location of trees: in phases. 5. Stock type: whips and standards. 6. Tree shelters: not used. 7. Weed control: none 8. Root depth: not assessed. 9. Methane: not assessed. 10. Landscape value: poor. 11. Other: Example of poor silvicultural practice leading to poor growth.
Desborough, Northamptonshire. Closed (c 1984) Grid ref: SP820846	No cover soil. >1 m of non-engineered, but highly compact boulder clay	1985	Common alder Italian alder Red alder Ash English oak Scots pine Sitka spruce Sycamore	Moderate Poor	1. Size of site: 3 ha. 2. Landform: slightly domed. 3. Tree coverage: 80%. 4. Location of trees: whole site. 5. Stock type: whips. 6. Tree shelters: not used. 7. Weed control: none 8. Root depth: not assessed. 9. Methane: not assessed. 10. Landscape value: poor-moderate. 11. Other: Example of poor silvicultural practice leading to poor growth.
Brixworth, Northamptonshire. Closed (c 1988) Grid ref: SP755716	No soil cover Approximately 1 m dry, compact boulder clay	1989	Red alder Beech Birch English oak	Poor Failed	1. Size of site: 1 ha. 2. Landform: slightly sloping. 3. Tree coverage: 1%. 4. Location of trees: in principle, whole site. 5. Stock type: whips 6. Tree shelters: some rabbit guards.

Site details	Soil capping: depth and type	Planting date	Tree species	Performance	Additional information
					7. Weed control: none.
					8. Root depth: not assessed.
					9. Methane: not assessed.
					10. Landscape value: none.
					11. Other: Example of poor silvicultural practice leading to total failure. Nearby restoration to grass, excellent.
Elsenham Quarry, Elsenham, Essex. Operational Grid ref: TL546268	Maximum of 1.5 m loose-tipped chalky boulder clay or sand screenings (sandy silt loam) Underlain by 10–20 cm of boulder clay (cap?)	1986	Ash Cherry Common alder Corsican pine Italian alder Red alder	Good	1. Size of site: 30 ha. 2. Landform: slightly domed. 3. Tree coverage: 10%. 4. Location of trees: 3 ridges (30 m wide). 5. Stock type 1+1 or 1+2 transplant. 6. Tree shelters: not used. 7. Weed control: for 3 years as necessary. 8. Root depth: maximum 1.4 m, average 0.91 m. 9. Methane: none detected. 10. Landscape value: excellent. 11. Other: Loose tipped soil encouraged good root growth, better in the sand than clay.

Appendix 2

Common and scientific names of tree species

ALDER	
Common*	*Alnus glutinosa*
Grey	*Alnus incana*
Italian	*Alnus cordata*
Red	*Alnus rubra*
APPLE	*Malus* spp.
Crab*	*Malus sylvestris*
ASH*	*Fraxinus excelsior*
ASPEN*	*Populus tremula*
BEECH*	*Fagus sylvatica*
BIRCH	
Downy*	*Betula pubescens*
Silver*	*Betula pendula*
CEDAR	*Cedrus* spp.
CHERRY	
Bird*	*Prunus padus*
Wild (Gean)*	*Prunus avium*
COCKSPUR THORN	*Crataegus crus-galli*
CYPRESS	*Cupressus* spp.
ELDER	*Sambucus nigra*
FALSE ACACIA	*Robinia pseudoacacia*
FALSE CYPRESS	*Chamaecyparis* spp.
FIR	
Douglas	*Pseudotsuga menzeisii*
Silver	*Abies alba*
HAWTHORN*	*Crataegus monogyna*
HAZEL*	*Corylus avellana*
HOLLY*	*Ilex aquifolium*
HORNBEAM*	*Carpinus betulus*
HORSE CHESTNUT	*Aesculus hippocastanum*
INDIAN BEAN TREE	*Catalpa* spp.
LARCH	
European	*Larix europaea*
Japanese	*Larix kaempferi*
LEYLAND CYPRESS	*Cupressocyparis leylandii*
LIME	
Caucasian	*Tilia* x *euchlora*
Small leafed*	*Tilia cordata*
LONDON PLANE	*Platanus* x *hispanica*
MAPLE	
Field*	*Acer campestre*
Norway	*Acer platanoides*
Red	*Acer rubrum*
Silver	*Acer saccharinum*
Sugar	*Acer saccharum*
MIDLAND THORN*	*Crataegus laevigata*
MULBERRY†	*Morus nigra*
White†	*Morus alba*
OAK	
Burr	*Quercus macrocarpa*

English (Pedunculate)*	*Quercus robur*
Pin	*Quercus palustris*
Red	*Quercus rubra*
Sessile*	*Quercus petraea*
Turkey	*Quercus cerris*
PINE	
Austrian	*Pinus nigra* var *austriaca*
Bishop	*Pinus muricata*
Corsican	*Pinus nigra* var *maritima*
Lodgepole	*Pinus contorta*
Longleaf	*Pinus palustris*
Monterey	*Pinus radiata*
Scots*	*Pinus sylvestris*
White	*Pinus strobus*
POPLAR	
White†	*Populus alba*
Balsam†	*Populus balsamifera*
Grey†	*Populus canescens*
ROWAN*	*Sorbus aucuparia*
SCOTS LABURNUM†	*Laburnum alpinum*
SOUTHERN BEECH	*Nothofagus procera*
SPINDLE TREE	*Euonymus europaeus*
SPRUCE	
Norway†	*Picea abies*
Sitka	*Picea sitchensis*
SWEET CHESTNUT†	*Castanea sativa*
SYCAMORE†	*Acer pseudoplatanus*
TULIP TREE	*Liriodendron tulipifera*
WALNUT†	*Juglans regia*
WESTERN HEMLOCK	*Tsuga heterophylla*
WESTERN RED CEDAR	*Thuja plicata*
WHITEBEAM*	*Sorbus aria*
Swedish†	*Sorbus intermedia*
WILLOW	
Almond leaved	*Salix triandra*
Bay*	*Salix pentandra*
Common osier	*Salix viminalis*
Crack*	*Salix fragilis*
Goat (Grey)	*Salix capraea*
Purple osier	*Salix purpurea*
Violet	*Salix daphnoides*
White*	*Salix alba*
YEW	*Taxus baccata*

*Generally accepted as truly native. †Introduced before 1600 (Mitchell, 1981).

Appendix 3

List of organisations consulted during compilation of this report

Agricultural Development and Advisory Service
ARC (South Western) Ltd
Aspinwall and Company
Avon County Council
Bain Aggregates Ltd
Banks Development Division
Barnsley Metropolitan Borough Council
Bedfordshire County Council
BFI Packington Ltd
Biffa Waste Services Ltd
Black Country Urban Forestry Unit
Blue Circle Industries Ltd
Bolton Metropolitan Borough Council
Boyer and Sons Ltd
Bradford Metropolitan Borough Council
Brett Gravel Ltd
Buckinghamshire County Council
Building Research Establishment
Bury Metropolitan Borough Council
Butterley Aggregates Ltd
Calderdale Metropolitan Borough Council
Cambridgeshire County Council
Chambers Waste Disposal Ltd
Cheshire County Council
Cleanaway Ltd
Cleveland County Council
Clwyd County Council
Cornwall County Council
Corporation of London
Cumbria County Council
Derbyshire County Council
Devon County Council
Dorset County Council
Dudley Metropolitan Borough Council
Durham County Council
Dyfed County Council
East Sussex County Council
ECC Construction Materials Ltd
Energy Technology Support Unit
Evered Bardon plc
Exmoor National Park
Foster Yeoman Ltd
Gateshead Metropolitan Borough Council
Gloucestershire County Council
Gloucestershire Sand and Gravel Ltd
Greenham Construction Materials Ltd
Greater Manchester Countryside Unit
Greater Manchester Minerals and Waste
 Disposal Planning Unit
Great Western Community Forest
Groundwork Trust
Grundon Ltd
Gwynedd County Council
Hales Waste Control Ltd
Hall Aggregates (Eastern Counties) Ltd
Hall Aggregates (South Coast) Ltd
Hampshire County Council
Hemmings Waste Management Ltd
Hertfordshire County Council
Hills Aggregates Ltd
Holderness Aggregates Ltd
ICI Chemicals and Polymers Ltd
Kent County Council
Kirklees Metropolitan Borough Council

Knox Associates
Lancashire County Council
Land Research Associates
Leeds City Council
Leigh Environment (Southern) Ltd
London Borough of Barnet
London Borough of Bexley
London Borough of Bromley
London Borough of Croydon
London Borough of Ealing
London Borough of Enfield
London Borough of Harrow
London Borough of Sutton
Lothian Regional Council
MRM Partnership
National Rivers Authority
Newcastle-upon-Tyne City Council
New Soils Ltd
Nickolls Quarries Ltd
Northamptonshire County Council
Northumberland County Council
North Yorkshire County Council
North Yorkshire Moors National Park
NSM Waste Control Ltd
Ogwyr Borough Council
Oldham Metropolitan Borough Council
Oxfordshire County Council
Peak District National Park
Premier Site Landfill
Redland Aggregates Ltd
RMC Ltd
Rochdale Metropolitan Borough Council
Ryton Gravel Co. Ltd
Sandsfield Gravel Co. Ltd
Scottish Aggregates Ltd
Shanks & McEwan (Waste Services) Ltd
Smith & Sons (Bletchington) Ltd
Snowdonia National Park
Solihull Metropolitan Borough Council
South Glamorgan County Council
South Tyneside Metropolitan Borough Council
Staffordshire County Council
St Albans Sand & Gravel Co. Ltd
Suffolk County Council
Summerleaze Ltd
Sunderland Metropolitan Borough Council
Surrey County Council
Taff-Ely Borough Council
Tarmac Econowaste Ltd
Trafford Metropolitan Borough Council
Tudor Griffiths Group
Wakefield Metropolitan Borough Council
Walsall Metropolitan Borough Council
Warwickshire County Council
Waste Management Ltd
Western Aggregates Ltd
West Sussex County Council
West Yorkshire Waste Management
Wiltshire County Council
W & M Thompson Earthworks Ltd
WRc
Yorkshire Dales National Park

Index

Printed in the United Kingdom for HMSO.
Dd.0294848, 2/93, C10, 3396/4, 5673, 226403.